Leonardo
Up Close and
Personal

Leonardo
Up Close and Personal

VICTORIA LOOSELEAF

BALLANTINE BOOKS ● NEW YORK

A Ballantine Book
Published by The Ballantine Publishing Group

www.randomhouse.com/BB/

Library of Congress Cataloging-in-Publication Data
Looseleaf, Victoria.
    Leonardo: up close and personal/Victoria Looseleaf.—1st ed.
        p. cm.
    Filmography: p.
    ISBN 0-345-43222-3 (alk. paper)
    1. DiCaprio, Leonardo.   I. Title.
PN2287.D4635L66   1998
791.43'028'092—dc21
    [B]   98-38013
                                                                CIP

Interior design by Michaelis/Carpelis Design Assoc. Inc.
Cover photo courtesy of Photofest
Cover inset photos courtesy of Victoria Looseleaf
Cover design by Min Choi

Manufactured in the United States of America

First Edition: October 1998

10 9 8 7 6 5 4 3 2 1

This book is dedicated to the memory of Lindsay Evalin Stark—teenage prophet and angel among us—as well as to my beloved brother, Richie.

Acknowledgments

The author would like to thank her best friends, Barbara Libbin and Vaughan T. Bennett, photographer Gary Leonard, and *Los Angeles Times* dance critic, Lewis Segal. Thanks also to Darius James, Robert Rosen, Bud Cort, Russ Butler, Jon Stolzberg, Sonja Wagner, Renee Barkan, Jim Harp, James Goldman, Jason Walker, Craig Urquhart, John Fleck, Kenny Zrubek, Barbara Simon, J. V. McCauley, Gigi Gullihur, Michelle Anton, Antonio Mejias-Rentas, Marc H. Glick, Ivan Moffat, Dr. Irwin Miller, Wendy Colton, Linda Lane, and the inimitable Mike Mollett.

Many thanks also to the DiCaprio family, without whom this book would not have been possible.

Special thanks to my wonderful editor, Cathy Repetti, and all of the terrific people at Ballantine, including Betsy Flagler, Min Choi, Cindy Berman, and Jie Yang. Thanks also to agents extraordinaire, Sandy Choron and Madeline Morel.

Huge hugs and kisses to my family, including brothers Brian and Gary, sister Kathy, mother Bernice, stepmother Esther, and, most notably, my father, F.A.W., my favorite Oscar date.

Contents

Leo, I Love Ya!

Yes, it's true; there are already a number of books on the market about Leonardo DiCaprio. Why not? He's the hottest actor on the planet. And for those of you out there who adore Leonardo, you may indeed know some of the lore behind the legendary golden-haired boy.

But I have actually known Leo and his family for more than half of his life, and the stories that I'm sharing here are the stories that will help you understand the real Leonardo DiCaprio. Because when people discover that I know Hollywood's hottest heartthrob, they invariably ask me, "What is he really like?"

Only my book will give you a rare glimpse into Leo, his family, and his friends from a unique viewpoint. Trust me: The Leo I know is a lot of things—from warm and adventurous to shy and introspective. But he's always been himself. And since he walked into my life with his father, George, and stepmother, Peggy, as a gangly youngster in the mid-eighties, he has proven himself to be bright, energetic, charming, generous, fun-loving, and even a little unpredictable.

I've watched him grow from an adorable little boy to a sexy, charismatic man; from a double-jointed adolescent who did strange things with his shoulders to the biggest star in the world. I've seen him at play and I've seen him at work.

But he's still just Leo to me—a great guy with a huge appetite for life and a huge talent that will continue to affect millions of people for a long, long time to come. When he made his first television talk show appearance on my show, *The Looseleaf Report,* I predicted that overnight he would be "a huge sensation—and girls were gonna go nuts!"

And so it has come to pass. While everything has changed, nothing has changed, because, Leo, you're the greatest—and I'll always love ya! Here, then, is a tribute to my friend Leonardo DiCaprio.

CHAPTER ONE

How Cool Is That?

T he stars seem to have been in perfect alignment on November 11, 1974, when Leonardo Wilhelm DiCaprio first made his presence known, entering this world as a beautiful blond baby boy. Actually, Leo made his presence known several months before.

While pregnant with Leo, his mother, Irmelin, was visiting Florence's famous Uffizi Gallery with her husband, George, when she felt a firm kick from her unborn baby as the couple looked at a painting by the great Renaissance master Leonardo da Vinci. The pair took this as a sign and—voilà—they decided to name their son Leonardo.

A masterpiece was born!

Irmelin Idenbirken came from Germany, but moved to the United States as a young girl. She met George DiCaprio—whose Italian surname means "from Capri"—in college in New York. The two fell in love and were married. Deciding they could further their hopes and dreams in California, the couple moved to Los Angeles shortly before Leonardo's birth.

Hollywood may symbolize glamour and glitz, but for the youthful DiCaprios, money was scarce and things were a constant struggle for the new family. Their first apartment was far from the hills of Beverly and the sweet ocean air of Malibu, but was instead in one of the seedier parts of Hollywood.

Leo's first home: the Garfield Avenue apartment

Garfield Avenue just north of Hollywood Boulevard near Western was home to prostitutes and drug addicts. Leonardo has said that Hollywood was not the kind of place ideally suited to raise a child.

George prefers to remember the old neighborhood as "colorful," recounting many nights spent on the boulevard with baby Leo in tow, trying to get the active baby to fall asleep. "It was crazy back then," George says. "The whole area was kind of like a red-light district. We lived opposite the poet Charles Bukowski, whose life was depicted in the movie *Barfly*. I knew him very well, and a lot of funny things happened with him. If he hadn't have died, who knows what he might have written—maybe even about Leonardo. Better yet, Leonardo might star in a Bukowski-based film some day."

With Leonardo's energy and zest for life, it's no wonder that, even as a baby, he had a hard time falling asleep. As George explains: "There would be many a balmy Hollywood night when I would be sitting in a big, creaky rocking chair, singing to Leonardo and rocking him, hoping he would fall asleep. He calmed down, but he wouldn't close his little eyes. He did fall asleep, though, if I walked around with him on my arm and we witnessed enough mayhem."

Mayhem, in this case, was ambulances arriving at the nearby massage parlors to pick up a patron or two who might have had a stroke or coronary while receiving a massage. "I'd wrap Leonardo in a blanket," George says, "and walk around the corner with him under my arm. We'd watch some poor guy with a coat over his head—so no one would recognize him—be hauled out on a gurney. I'd meet Bukowski out there, and after they'd take these guys away, we'd walk around a bit more before I would go home and put Leonardo in his little crib in the front room. He would finally nod off!"

But it wasn't sleep—or lack of it—that finally broke up the DiCaprios' marriage. It was financial pressure.

Shortly before Leonardo's first birthday, George and Irmelin were divorced. But they remained friends and were determined to raise Leonardo in a warm, supportive environment. It was two households now, instead of one, with Leonardo spending most of the time with his mom, but many weekends with his father—and stepmother, Peggy—who lived nearby.

Leonardo may have been the product of a broken home, but the effects for him were rather positive. He always had wonderful relationships with both parents.

It was these feelings of security and being loved that contributed to Leonardo's positive and confident attitude. He truly enjoyed being around people and has always been a natural poser for the camera. And unlike many other little boys, Leonardo adored being well groomed and dressed up.

Long hair also seemed to run in the family. Indeed, George has had long hair and a beard for his entire adult life, so for haircuts, which were not that frequent, George took little

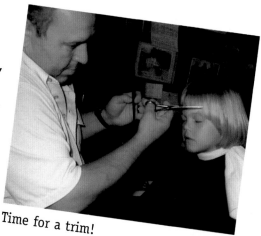

Time for a trim!

Leo to a local barber. Leonardo loved jumping up in the chair and sitting patiently while his straight-edged bangs were trimmed to perfection.

Other patrons would remark on how well-mannered Leonardo was, not to mention that beautiful face! But Leonardo would be quite adamant, actually, that the barber cut only a little each time. He wasn't quite convinced that his hair would always grow back!

While much has been said of Leo's upbringing, especially the fact that his parents were not made in a middle class mold, his background has appeared to work in Leonardo's favor. The fact that both George and Irmelin were very liberal, indeed, ex-hippie types, whose friends were artists, musicians, authors and yes, dreamers, has instilled in Leo a firm belief that "anything is entirely possible."

Leo and stepbrother Adam

Growing up in the seventies was actually a very cool thing for young Leo. His father certainly had one of the hipper jobs around: he distributed underground comic books for a living. This was unheard of to most people. But to the DiCaprios, it was a way of life, with George often entertaining such comic-book luminaries as Robert Crumb and Harvey Pekar.

Hubert (Cubby) Selby, Jr., the author of *Last Exit to Brooklyn*, was also a frequent guest in the DiCaprio abode. Cubby once gave the young Leonardo a tiny set of boxing gloves as a gift, but boxing was not in the cards for the boy with the finely chiseled features and sparkly blue-green eyes. And Leo, as it happens, didn't care about the gift.

L E O N A R D O
UP CLOSE AND PERSONAL

Part of George's job included going to local bookstores and arranging public readings for beat poets like William Burroughs and Allen Ginsberg (both now deceased). The sixties radical, Abbie Hoffman, could also often be found visiting the DiCaprio household. In fact, one of Leonardo's early childhood friends was America Hoffman, son of Abbie and Anita.

What was important was far more than the pleasures that money could buy. It was the idea that Leo was exposed to the creative arts at a very early age, and that he discovered he could be open to new experiences. While other kids' parents may have kept them on tight leashes and schedules, Leo's parents were the opposite. Young Leo was given the freedom and opportunity to explore.

The DiCaprios' former Los Feliz home

Leonardo remembers his dad as a bohemian who was in the thick of the underground artist scene. George imparted a lot of unique values to Leo. Some of those values had to do with sex. George was open and frank with his son, which probably accounts for Leonardo's inherently probing nature and curiosity. Today George describes his son's personality as a kind of quirky Don Quixote type: "Leo is on a quest to find out how many things he can do in life."

One of the things young Leo did not enjoy was doing homework. But Leo does love to tell the story about how his father used to show him all of his rare comic books that were strewn around the house and stored in the garage. Leo's insatiable appetite for discovery was a big one. He often devoured those books and comics.

Leonardo loved the Checkered Demon comic book and even wore his

Leo and stepmother, Peggy, waiting for the Pope

Checkered Demon T-shirt until it was nearly threadbare. One day in 1986, the Pope himself was coming to downtown Los Angeles and Leonardo was excited at the thought of seeing him. It was going to be a real event, George had explained to his young son, with thousands of people lining the streets to get a glimpse of this very famous man who did not come to the United States often, much less to Los Angeles.

Although Leo did not personally get an audience with His Holiness, he was happy to be outdoors on a beautiful day, posing for the camera in his most favorite T-shirt!

George took Leonardo virtually everywhere he felt would enrich his son's mind, from poetry readings and movies to music concerts, outdoor street festivals, and art museums. Indeed, Leonardo would later become a collector of contemporary artists, like Robt. Williams, an old family friend and Leonardo's godfather, whose unique work is a blend of cartoonish art that has been exhibited in museums.

It was George, in fact, who first took ten-year-old Leonardo to a performance festival and encouraged his son to go on-stage. Leonardo, wearing a red jumpsuit, soon found himself dancing, his long blond hair flying, in front of a cheering audience. George finally had to pull him off the stage.

Leonardo loved dressing up, showing an early tendency toward creating different characters—another reason, perhaps, to become an actor. Leonardo not only got to dress up in all kinds of interesting and exotic costumes but would get paid for doing it, too!

When money was tight, however, Halloween, the ultimate time for dressing up in a child's life, would have to be improvised. Leonardo would don a zebra-striped mask, a bolt of animal-skin cloth would be wrapped around him

Tarzan-style, and the final touch, a red cape, would be tied around his neck. At a very young age, Leo was not exactly King of the World, but he certainly was King of the Jungle, or at least King of His Neighborhood!

Another way Leo liked dressing up—or

The Los Angeles Mudpeople

dressing down—was as a member of the Los Angeles Mudpeople. The Mudpeople are a group of urban primitives led by teacher and poet Mike Mollett. Mike organizes walkabouts, in which friends cake their nearly naked bodies with wet mud, adorning themselves with leaves and other organic materials and finally donning huge handmade mud heads.

They do not speak, but walk around various parts of Los Angeles "exploring" their terrain: meaning they inspect anything from loose street gravel to blooming bougainvillea to somebody's shiny belt buckle.

George and Peggy liked being Mudpeople and they thought Leo might enjoy it, too. I was never a Mudperson but preferred taking pictures of them instead on their many outings. A favorite Mudpeople excursion was participating in the annual Festival of Masks. Leo "mudded up" with George, Peggy, Mike, and the others before they all marched in the parade down Wilshire Boulevard.

Hey, it was probably just another form of acting. But Leo excelled at it. He would remain speechless for a while, march around unself-consciously, and ultimately be in awe of his surroundings.

While mudding up took a bit of doing, being a natural clown was a lot easier for Leonardo. He had a mischievous side and would continue to hone it in the years to come, when he entertained cast and crew on the many movie sets he would work on.

I remember one party that I gave in a Chinese restaurant where he folded his napkin into a samurai-warrior kind of hat, then stuck it on his head. It would have been okay if the napkin were clean,

Samurai Leo

but his was covered in duck sauce! Little Leo, we all soon realized, took after his father, who also liked joking around.

Leo also liked goofing around at Pasadena's annual Doo Dah Parade, a kind of spoof on parades in general. Whether posing with weird parade marchers or striking a stance himself in

Father and son goofing off

attention-grabbing style, Leo would always have a great time, no matter the occasion.

To put it bluntly, Leonardo's early upbringing was never dull. But having very hip parents, the young Leo also found that he had nothing to rebel against. His parents' liberal and all-encompassing lifestyle and beliefs made adolescent rebellion moot. Leo figured he would leave the revolution to his folks.

Tradition, though, was not totally foreign to the DiCaprio household. Leo, like most young kids growing up, had a great love of animals and pets. Leo was the proud owner of a pet cat, Germain. It was a sad day when Germain died in a fight with another cat.

Leo poses with a Doo Dah parade participant

Undaunted, Leo brought home a couple of frogs he found in a swamp and put them in a cage. Innocently, when Leo was cleaning the cage one day, he put the frogs in a bowl and, to prevent the amphibians from jumping out, covered it tightly with plastic wrap.

Bad move, Leo! The frogs died.

Leo also loved going fishing with his father and family friends off the coast of California. He didn't exactly like the idea of "hurting" the fish, though, and then eating it, because fish was not his favorite food. In any case, he absolutely would not take part in cleaning the fish. But

Leonardo certainly enjoyed being on the water and reeling in a big one. Indeed, he was most proud of his efforts, as he delighted in showing off his catch.

For years his profound interest in the sea continued. (A good thing, as his future *Titanic* success would require that he have a very close relationship to water at that point in his life!) In fact, there was a time when Leo considered studying oceanography. That career, as we all know, went by the wayside, but Leo found it in his heart to make generous contributions to a fund aimed at saving Florida's manatees.

As he grew, Leo often would talk of wanting to explore all kinds of animal life, especially in exotic places. He has a particular interest in endangered animals.

Leonardo's most favorite animal was

George and Leo show off their big catch

Leo and Rocky

his dog. A rottweiler, appropriately named Rocky, who had been the runt of the litter, came into young Leo's life and became one of his best friends. Leo really loved that dog. Unfortunately, Rocky was diagnosed as epileptic and began having seizures. Leonardo was so devoted to Rocky, though, that he began doing research on the subject of canine epilepsy, eventually administering medication to the dog himself.

"We were sentimental about Rocky," George recalled, "and then he got cancer of the throat. We held on to him, though, and spent thousands of dollars. We eventually had to put him down when he was nine years old."

Leonardo seemed to have better luck with his pet lizard, Blizz, as no misfortune came to him.

Leo's true calling in life did not lie with animals or with alternative lifestyles. But his bright eyes would be opened wide when his stepbrother, Adam Starr, the son of George's second wife, Peggy, made $50,000 for doing a Golden Grahams breakfast cereal commercial. Leonardo must have thought, "How cool is *that!*"

The Los Feliz house Leo calls home

Leo Rising... and Shining

It would be a while, however, before Leonardo would be making tens of thousands of dollars. But not that long. In truth, Leonardo had actually thought about becoming a television star several years before Adam made his first commercial: It was at the ripe old age of five when the precocious boy made his small-screen debut on the children's TV show *Romper Room*. It was his favorite show.

Things didn't exactly work out. Little Leo was ejected from the set for his "uncontrollable behavior."

Time was on Leonardo's side, though. And Leonardo was happy just being a kid, doing the stuff that normal kids do. His mother had moved to a house in Los Feliz; George and Peggy also took up residence in the area that would eventually be one of L.A.'s more trendy places to live and hang out.

Currently, Madonna lives there; Gwen Stefani, who fronts the group No Doubt, recently moved into a Mediterranean manse; and the Red Hot Chili Peppers' lead singer, Flea, also has digs in the area. There are also lots of cool boutiques, bookstores, coffee shops, and nightclubs that Leo still frequents today. He could never give up his old neighborhood. In actuality, it seems like the 'hood is catching up to him!

After Adam's commercial aired, he landed a recurring role in a network television series *Battlestar Galactica*, short-lived as it was. But this really put the acting bee in Leo's bonnet. The DiCaprios were inspired to take the next step.

As it happened, Irmelin had a friend who worked at Harry Gold's talent agency. Leonardo was taken in to do a reading and—no surprise—he was really good. The agent wanted Leonardo to change his name, though, to something less ethnic—Lenny Williams. But the determined young boy refused. Leonardo stuck to his guns and soon began going out on auditions. There wasn't exactly a pot of gold at the end of the rainbow his first few times out.

After an audition where he'd suffered yet another humiliating rejection—"wrong haircut!" (and this was after he'd stopped getting Prince Charming bowl cuts from his local barber!)—father and son had a talk.

Leonardo was blue and questioning his career move.

George, ever the loving, wise, patient father, told his son to relax and wait it out.

The laid-back attitude had served George well. It would do the same for young Leonardo. Something clicked, and in the two years between the ages of fourteen and sixteen, Leonardo made about twenty TV commercials, including ones for Matchbox cars and other toys, bubble gum, and breakfast cereals. He also began making educational films. At age fifteen Leonardo was in a short film made for the Disney TV show *Mickey's Safety Club*. He was also featured in another public service announcement, "How to Deal with a Parent Who Takes Drugs."

While the money, which was his initial drive to get into acting, did make things easier for all of the DiCaprios, making television commercials wasn't enough to satisfy Leo's inventive streak. He hungered for the chance to create a true character, one that lived, breathed, and emoted for more than thirty seconds or a minute.

Of course, many people wait years before getting their

big break. Leo's was seemingly just around the corner. Following the educational films were guest appearances on several television series. He played a boy gone wrong on *The New Adventures of Lassie,* along with roles on *Roseanne* and in a short-lived series, *The Outsiders,* based on the Brat Pack movie of the same name directed by Francis Ford Coppola.

It was becoming apparent that the good-looking boy was not just another pretty Hollywood face. If only he could get the chance to develop his talent in a longer format. He got that chance. Leonardo nailed a spot on the TV soap opera *Santa Barbara,* portraying a teenage alcoholic.

While some people make long careers out of soap operas, Leonardo, when finally given the opportunity to sink his acting chops into a gritty character, found the daily routine of soap opera work and the on-the-set school tutoring confining and tedious.

Since he was only fifteen, the law allowed him to be on the set for just half the working day, yet he still had huge amounts of dialogue to prepare. While he received tutoring on the set, school had never really been Leonardo's primary passion. He did attend John Marshall High School for a short time, but ended up receiving a G.E.D. (graduate equivalency diploma), instead of graduating with classmates. But Leonardo's mind was nimble, his nature restless.

After only a few months on *Santa Barbara,* he was again

John Marshall High School

looking for steady work. Several auditions and callbacks later, Leonardo landed a recurring role in the TV series *Parenthood*. A sitcom spin-off from the 1989 hit movie of the same name, this was a prime-time NBC show, with Leonardo featured among a regular cast.

Leonardo played Garry Buckman, yet another of several troubled teens in his career. The show was canceled after thirteen episodes.

While audiences had loved the movie *Parenthood*, starring Steve Martin and directed by Ron Howard, far fewer were wild about the weekly TV show, whose cast was not that recognizable. Again Leonardo was without work.

But again it was not for long. As soon as one job ended, another one materialized. Leonardo's biggest break to date came on the TV series *Growing Pains*. It was 1991 and Leonardo was cast as a young homeless boy, Luke Brower. It was thought that Leonardo could be brought in to revitalize the teen market, the show's biggest audience in the eighties, when its star, Kirk Cameron, was at the height of his popularity.

In its seventh year, *Growing Pains* needed the shot in the arm that Leonardo could give it. His character, Luke, moved in with the Seavers family, and many issues surrounding the young homeless in America could be brought to light each week.

Leonardo, besides relishing the steady work and the very nice paycheck, also liked the idea of filming *Growing Pains* in front of a live studio audience. It was like performing in a play. Of course, as was the case with the dialogue he had to utter on *Santa Barbara,* he wasn't always thrilled with the writing on the show.

An interesting trend began to develop at around this time. Leonardo was starting to get written up in teen magazines. Photo spreads promoting both *Parenthood* and *Growing Pains* tended to focus on Leonardo, as he seemed to stand out from the other actors. Whether it was for his wholesome and exceptional good looks or his on-set pranks and joking personality, he was getting noticed.

Irmelin's involvement in her son's career took a new turn as she worked to get him coverage in the fanzines. Leonardo's ever-increasing exposure was a source of pride and pleasure back then, as well as an indication that his career was really going places. Irmelin has collected, over the years, tens of thousands of Leonardo's fan letters, along with a huge array of scripts.

Growing Pains was soon to be a thing of the past, though. In spite of Leonardo's efforts—he did appear in twenty-four episodes—the show was canceled the following season. There had been talk of Leo's character getting picked up for his own series, but this was not to be. The learning experiences proved invaluable, however.

Leonardo discovered a lot about himself while working on the series. He came to realize that he was brave enough to cry on camera. He also got to work on his comic timing, something he has yet to fully explore, but something he will, no doubt, be great at.

Acting with Kirk Cameron also proved helpful. Kirk had gone through a period as a teen idol and knew how to handle it. More important, he was there for Leo to offer advice and supportive words.

As Leonardo was growing up, and growing more good looking, people would tell him "You look like River

Phoenix," or "You're going to be the next Johnny Depp."

This was both positive and negative feedback for the youth. He didn't like labels and he didn't always appreciate comparisons. Still, the attention was a boost.

It would be a while before Hollywood would officially declare Leonardo DiCaprio their reigning box-office star, but when it happened, it was going to be major. First, however, Leo had to make a good movie.

Although many publications, as well as Leonardo's film-going audience, like to credit Leonardo's cinematic debut with his breakout appearance in *This Boy's Life,* he first acted—if one can call it such—in the schlock-fest movie *Critters 3.* The year was 1991 and young Leo, just before winning the Luke Brower role on *Growing Pains,* battled small fur-ball invaders in a movie he would more than likely want to forget.

The latest in a line of B-movie sequels to the 1986 hit *Gremlins,* this creature feature's special effects were low-tech to the max. The alien fuzzballs looked more like the stuff a household pet might regurgitate, and the audience knew it. It was possibly one of the worst films of all time. Leonardo was billed as simply "Leonard DiCaprio" in this flick that went straight to video.

His next endeavor, *Poison Ivy,* was far superior, but it is altogether possible to miss the blond boy if you blink. A vehicle for Drew Barrymore, *Poison Ivy* featured young Leo in the small role of Guy, who was not much more than a billed extra. It is fun trying to find Leo, though, in this movie about a teenager who infiltrates a family with deadly results. (Hint: You can spot him in a group scene at the beginning of the film—but only for a few brief, shining moments!)

Needless to say, these aren't Leo's finest moments on the silver screen. But ever the trouper, he was about to experience his most important break.

What other teen actor could call Robert De Niro and Ellen Barkin costars so early in the acting game? While Leo would appear in nearly every scene in the movie *This Boy's Life,* the young actor's credit would read, most appropriately, "introducing Leonardo DiCaprio."

CHAPTER THREE

This Charmer's Life

Fear is not a dominant trait in Leonardo DiCaprio. It was his complete lack of fear, then, that no doubt propelled him to be so bold in his audition with the great actor Robert De Niro. Not being starstruck also helped. As Leo was already a working professional, he took the audition in stride, viewing it as a reading with "just another actor."

Right!

Leo wanted the part of Toby in the screen adaptation of Tobias Wolff's 1989 memoir, *This Boy's Life.* He knew he could do a great job in the story that revolves around the horrific experiences a young boy has to endure while growing up in a small town with his mother and nasty stepfather in the late 1950s. Oh, yeah, Leo wanted the part, but he wasn't going to obsess about it to the point where he would perform badly.

No way! Leo would do things, as he always had, in his own style. He stood in front of De Niro, pointed at his face, and screamed his lines. He showed guts and De Niro noticed.

Of course, it wasn't a cinch from the start. Scottish-born Michael Caton-Jones was slated to direct. No novice, he had already helmed the movie *Scandal,* a retelling of a true British political scandal, starring John Hurt and Bridget Fonda. The director also put his stamp on the World War II drama *Memphis Belle,* as well as the hit comedy, *Doc Hollywood,* starring another former teen idol, Michael J. Fox.

Caton-Jones knew that *This Boy's Life* would rest heavily on the shoulders of the actor chosen to play Toby. As it happens, Leonardo read for Caton-Jones early in the casting process, but the director was leery of going with Leo without seeing other actors. In all, Caton-Jones interviewed and auditioned over four hundred Hollywood hopefuls.

But it was Leonardo who performed with a natural brilliance and charisma that stuck in the director's mind.

Leonardo and his mother, Irmelin, happened to be vacationing in Germany when they learned that he had won the prized role. It was to be the launch of a major career.

At the beginning, the film seems like it could be a mother-son road picture, with Ellen Barkin and Leonardo, playing Carolyn and Toby, driving across the gorgeous tableau of the American Southwest. Shades of *Thelma and Louise,* perhaps, as they are on the run from Carolyn's latest physically abusive boyfriend. They've left Florida for Utah, but will soon head for the great Pacific Northwest.

It quickly becomes evident, however, that this will be an emotional roller coaster, with its three main stars delivering bravura performances in the process.

Filming of *This Boy's Life* took place in Vancouver, British Columbia, Utah, and in the tiny town of Concrete, Washington, a hundred miles northeast of Seattle, where author Tobias Wolff grew up. A great deal of work was put into re-creating the look of the late fifties. Leonardo also immersed himself in the part, sporting a crew cut and getting approval from the author, whom he met briefly while shooting in Concrete.

Leonardo, far from the Method acting school of De Niro, chose to keep their meeting brief. He wanted to keep a certain distance and play the part the only way he knew how—his way!

L E O N A R D O
U P   C L O S E   A N D   P E R S O N A L

As a guest on my television show, *The Looseleaf Report,*
in November of 1992, Leo and I talked about his experiences on the film, including a minor bicycle accident that
had the producers extremely worried.

"I was on a break one afternoon, so I jumped on my bike
to go for a ride," recounted Leo. "The next thing I knew, I
fell off and scraped my chin. The producers found out and
realized I couldn't work for a few days, which was going to
cost them about $250,000. So I picked off the scab and put
it in a bag and I sealed it." Leo laughed. "It became part of
the Leonardo DiCaprio Memorabilia Exhibition."

Leo was cool and casual, wearing a pukka-shell necklace,
plaid lumber jacket, T-shirt, and baggy pants. He also told
me that a lot of girls from Concrete were hanging around
his trailer. "In packs," he said jokingly, "and usually with
their mothers."

This prompted me to predict his future as a megastar.

Leo's first talk-show appearance

"Overnight you're going to turn into this huge sensation," I told him. "Girls are gonna go nuts."

Leo, in typically modest fashion, insisted: "We don't wanna say that, 'cause who knows, things can happen. The film can get destroyed." He added cannily, "It's not one of my favorite things to be recognized. If it gets to a certain level, it'll start to get annoying."

Leonardo as psychic. Even then his eyes were looking toward the stars. The film, as the world soon found out, did not get destroyed. And it was also the beginning of a friendship with De Niro, whom he used to call at home on a regular basis. Of course, Leo had been a big De Niro fan before the two worked together. Leo admitted to seeing the movie *Raging Bull* five or six times.

It also happened that during the filming of *This Boy's Life,* Leonardo was going through puberty—he shot up a full four inches! "It's puberty," he told me, "you deal with it."

on *The Looseleaf Report* in 1992

This boy dealt with it by having to crouch down during several of the scenes so he did not appear taller than De Niro.

The only other near catastrophe during the shooting, besides the quarter-million-dollar scab, was the one scene where De Niro gives Leo fist fighting lessons. After all, De Niro is an actor who played a professional boxer, so it wasn't a complete surprise that things got a little out of control.

Yeah, Leo was the recipient of a couple of choice-looking black-and-blue marks.

"I got a couple of bruises from big old Bobby D," Leonardo said with a smile. "But he was very careful and nice about it. People say things about him, that he stays in character between scenes. He didn't stay in character with me. He was really nice and considerate. He said to me: 'You did the most honest portrayal of the hundred people we tested for the role. You didn't have a lot of the mannerisms kids have today.' I just let it happen naturally," Leo admits, adding, "De Niro is kinda like a god to everybody."

All things considered, though, maybe Leo should have been more respectful of those little boxing gloves that author Cubby Selby, Jr., had given him those many years ago!

While much has been said of Leonardo's working relationship with De Niro, the youngster also got along tremendously well with Ellen Barkin. "She was supportive,"

Leo recalled. "She really taught me a lot. She had lived her life in the movies—she had gone through good and bad times—and it was an education working with her."

Barkin mentored Leonardo during their work together. But Leo drew parallels between his mother-son film relationship and his real-life one with his mother, Irmelin. Mother and son, as best friends and free spirits, was one of the themes of *This Boy's Life*. It's also true of Leo and Irmelin.

George, who hails from the same school of open-mindedness and free-thinking as Irmelin, and who gave Leo's film very high marks, remembers a particularly funny incident during the ten weeks of filming *This Boy's Life*. One afternoon George knocked on Caton-Jones's trailer door and was welcomed inside. He said that on the desk was a book, opened to reveal the title, *How To Direct*.

Wow! It must have worked, because Caton-Jones got masterful performances from his cast, especially with Leo's star-making turn.

When the film opened, Leonardo was singled out for his wonderful work. An emotional chord had been struck with audiences and critics in this tale of teenage angst.

David Ansen of *Newsweek* referred to the youngster as "the astonishingly talented Leonardo DiCaprio." Film critics Gene Siskel and Roger Ebert gave the film a rousing two thumbs up, with Siskel hailing Leonardo as "simply terrific." *People* magazine said, "Leonardo DiCaprio, in his first major movie role, carried the film with impressive ease, letting you see the hurt beneath this kid's affected toughness."

Leonardo's performance proved to be more than good. He even secured his first award for his performance in *This Boy's Life,* the New Generation Award from the Los Angeles Film Critics Association.

Leonardo was accepting of his notices with both a degree of wisdom and a smattering of reality.

Though *This Boy's Life* only grossed $4 to $5 million when it was released in the United States in 1993, the name of Leonardo DiCaprio, once thought to be too ethnic, was now the buzz of Hollywood insiders.

With his portrayal of Toby Wolff, Leonardo delivered the first important performance of his career. His work on the film also gave the young actor a peek into his own natural talents and abilities, as if he'd tapped into a deep vein that had previously been hidden. Leonardo understood for the first time that acting was less about money—his initial motivation—and more about feelings and raw emotions. He admitted, in fact, to being emotionally drained by the end of filming.

Leonardo was beginning to grow up, both on screen and off. The ease with which he faced a variety of situations would help him in the years to come. For now, though, he was getting a taste of living Hollywood-style. Movie stardom was not a given, but the offers were starting to roll in and Leonardo DiCaprio, in true winner's form, was going to seize the day.

He was also trying to seize the ball!

Leo loves baseball, and we used to go watch the Dodgers play at Chavez Ravine in Elysian Park during the summer. As loyal a Dodgers fan as Leo was, he could usually be found wearing baseball caps from a variety of teams, which didn't always sit well with some of the fans around us. Of course, I like to think that when we went to the game with my nephew, Barry, who was visiting from Florida at the time, Leo wore a Florida State cap in honor of him.

Barry, who was twelve to Leonardo's seventeen that summer of 1992, had recently decided he wanted to be an actor. I thought it would be cool to get the two boys together. Too bad the Dodgers weren't doing very well that season, which accounted for some of the empty seats. That was okay with us, though, because we liked to

Leo and pal Barry at Dodger Stadium

stretch out and make a mess eating everything Dodger Stadium could offer—peanuts, Dodger Dogs, cotton candy, ice cream, pretzels.

Yeah, Leo may have looked skinny and a bit underfed (later on he would even have a personal trainer to try and bulk up—to no avail) but he seriously liked to eat. Barry and I weren't doing any too shabbily, either. While scarfing down anything salty, sticky, and slurpy, Leonardo was dispensing helpful advice to Barry about acting.

"Be as natural as possible," Leonardo told Barry. "Try and make everything as natural as possible. And if you don't feel you're good, try to improve. The main thing is, it's gotta be real."

Wow! Barry getting acting tips from Leonardo was, to him, as cool as getting, say, hitting tips from Ken Griffey, Jr. Just then one of the Dodgers foul-tipped a pitch high into the stands. It was coming right for us, and since none of us had brought a mitt, and our hands were filled with food, we scrambled to avoid being hit.

Suddenly, a throng of kids trying to catch the errant ball surrounded us. One of them managed to snag the ball on its second or third bounce. The kid, about Leo's age, noticed the young actor.

"Hey, aren't you in *Growing Pains?* Would you autograph this ball for me?" he asked, a big grin on his face.

Leo obliged. But then it was back to business as usual—

more eating. There was pizza and fries and Cokes and licorice and more peanuts and more cotton candy. Ugh! By the seventh-inning stretch none of us was feeling too swift. Leonardo made a mad dash for the bathroom, with Barry following close behind. It seems the rising star wasn't quite able to hold his own in the junk-food department.

Well, it could have been worse. The Dodgers could have lost.

Come to think of it, they did!

While Leo was on his way to becoming a megastar, he wasn't the kind of person who would easily forget his friends. In fact, each summer, Leonardo looked forward to an annual Fourth of July party thrown by DiCaprio family friend artist Neal Taylor.

Taylor lived in a house in Hancock Park, an area that features beautiful mansions that used to be popular in the 1940s. Taylor's place, however, was in slight disrepair, which was all the better for big, wild, outdoor bashes. And Leo wasn't the only one who enjoyed these parties. We all loved the chow, the fireworks...and the good times.

After the barbecue, the kids moved on to firecrackers and sparklers.

We absolutely could not rein Leo in on the Fourth of July. Perhaps it was his patriotism. Then again, "It was just a fun way to party," he said, after lighting off a few rounds.

Leo sporting his favorite James Dean t-shirt at a family gathering

Peel Me a Grape

Leonardo had, at some point in time, wanted to study oceanography. With his high school equivalency diploma in hand, he had no plans, though, of going to either a senior prom or pursuing higher education. And, unlike other actors who had opted for college—Jodie Foster had gone to Yale and Claire Danes is headed there now—Leo knew college was not for him.

Instead of choosing what courses to take, Leonardo was choosing what movie he would make next. He mentioned on my television show, *The Looseleaf Report,* that he had wanted to do *Marvin's Room,* but "the deal wasn't done, so we better not talk about it."

Leo, superstitious? Perhaps. And though he eventually would do *Marvin's Room,* it was still three years away. Now he was, as they say in the business, "fielding offers."

Okay. Leo could go for the big bucks, or he could decide to do a project that really appealed to him. Money and fame would sound pretty good to most people. But Leo is not "most people." What a dilemma! He was up for parts in two movies, *Hocus Pocus* and *What's Eating Gilbert Grape?* He invested a lot of time and energy in the *Gilbert Grape* audition even though he was advised *Hocus Pocus* was the better project. After all, he could costar with Bette Midler and make more money.

How many people remember *Hocus Pocus?* Not many. That movie bombed at the box office. But we all remember *Gilbert Grape.*

Director Lasse Hallström was behind the Oscar-winning work *My Life As a Dog,* written by Peter Hedges. Hedges had written a quirky novel called *What's Eating Gilbert Grape?,* and Hallström knew this was the next picture he wanted to make.

It was to star two of Hollywood's hottest hot actors—

Johnny Depp and Juliette Lewis. The casting of Gilbert Grape's younger, mentally handicapped brother, Arnie, was a challenge.

But it was a role Leonardo felt he could handle. One that he could really stretch his acting abilities with. The director wasn't quite as convinced in the beginning.

Leonardo, in spite of the acclaim he'd received for *This Boy's Life*, was still required to audition, along with many other young actors in town.

Hallström didn't want someone good-looking for Arnie and was concerned that Leo's blond wholesomeness would distract the audience from the character's mental disabilities. But Leo rose to the occasion. For the first time in his career, he even indulged himself in researching the character like De Niro would have.

And he nailed the part.

Leo still did his homework. He traveled with Hallström to Texas and spent many days visiting homes for the mentally disabled, actually trying to get into their minds. He ended up meeting a young autistic man whom he eventually used as his model for the role, incorporating his own mannerisms into his portrayal.

Adding more authenticity to Arnie was his haircut ("a chili-bowl haircut"). Leonardo also wore a mouthpiece in order to give Arnie's face a slightly deformed look.

Ultimately, *Gilbert Grape* is a character-driven story. Johnny Depp plays Gilbert, a grocery-bagger by profession. Meanwhile, his obese mother hasn't left the house in seven years and his sisters are always fighting. To top things off, Gilbert is in charge of taking care of his seventeen-year-old mentally challenged brother, Arnie, who has a habit of climbing to the top of the town's water tower, which keeps the local police busy. When the fun-loving Becky (Juliette Lewis) enters Gilbert's life, the movie turns into a genuine and heartfelt experience.

The overwhelming surprise? Leonardo's amazing performance. What was meant to be a showcase for Johnny Depp turned into a tour de force for our boy Leo. And he loved every minute of it.

Depp, ten years older than Leonardo, provided support for the younger actor, much the way De Niro had. Leonardo took advantage of the situation by learning as much as he could from Depp, gleaning knowledge and skills, so as to allow him to broaden his range and deepen his own portrayals of characters.

Like the brothers in the movie, the two had a camaraderie off the set as well. The film was shot in Austin, Texas, which didn't have the most exciting night life in the world. The pair often took to amusing each other with weird facial expressions and pranks. They had a totally carefree buddy-buddy relationship.

Hallström had dubbed Leo "star material," and the critics agreed. Once more they were talking about Leo's incredible portrayal of a difficult character. Hal Hinson of *The Washington Post* exclaimed: "DiCaprio's characterization of Arnie is a marvelous, completely unself-conscious performance." *Entertainment Weekly* trumpeted: "Leonardo DiCaprio, the vibrant young star of *This Boy's Life,* gives an audacious and technically amazing performance as Arnie. This is one boy who commands your attention."

Even the most sacrosanct of newspapers, *The New York Times,* raved about Leo: "He winds up capturing the enormous range of Arnie's emotions and making it clear why the Grape brothers share such an unbreakable bond. The performance has a sharp, desperate intensity from beginning to end."

Our boy Leo was destined for greatness. In 1994 he again received the Los Angeles Film Critics Association New Generation Award, as well as a National Board of Review Award. But best of all, his performance had been so authoritative and unique that the Academy of Motion Picture Arts and Sciences awarded him with a nomination.

In February of 1994, Leonardo's name was included in the category of Best Supporting Actor. His name would go down in history beside the other nominees: Ralph Fiennes, Tommy Lee Jones, John Malkovich, and Peter Postlethwaite.

Leonardo, needless to say, was extremely excited. And terrified! Yes, the thought of having to perhaps stand up and deliver an acceptance speech while the whole world was watching did not appeal to him. He had always been nervous speaking in front of large audiences. Still, he didn't think he'd win.

But before he could think about going to the ceremonies, he was having to think about what to wear! In recent years, the Oscars, in addition to awarding gold statuettes for talent, had become a fantastic fashion show, with stars being courted by big-name designers. Leonardo was now on that list. While many designers made their pitches to Leo, he ultimately decided on wearing Armani. Why not? Giorgio Armani himself called Leo from Milan, offering his clothes.

It was an offer he couldn't refuse. Not bad for someone who spent most of his life in comfy old T-shirts, jeans, and baseball caps!

Oscar night was a production of a different sort. Leonardo attended the ceremonies with his father, his stepmother, and his mother. He was nervous, nonetheless. But the award was not to be. It went to Tommy Lee Jones for his role in *The Fugitive*. As Leo wasn't even expecting a nomination, he wasn't too disappointed at not winning his first time out. But his star was sailing high, and Leo's life would never be the same again.

Not yet twenty, Leo was experiencing things foreign to most people, even veteran actors. Leo still had his wits about him, for sure. The golden-haired boy was able to maintain his humility and still have a great time. He was still, when all was said and done, just a kid from East Hollywood.

That's definitely the Leo I know!

CHAPTER FIVE

He Got Game...and Guns

With his 1994 Oscar nomination under his belt, the world was at Leo's feet. After the hot young actor River Phoenix died tragically of a drug overdose outside of Johnny Depp's Sunset Strip nightclub, the Viper Room, Hollywood needed an immediate replacement for its emotionally intense antihero type. Phoenix had been tapped to star in the film version of Anne Rice's *Interview with the Vampire*.

Now this was a role Leo could really sink his teeth into. He felt bad about Phoenix, although the two actors had never met. But the show, as they say, must go on. And *Interview with the Vampire* would go on without Leonardo DiCaprio. His name was mentioned around town as a possible contender and he did audition for the part, impressing the director, Neil Jordan, and producer David Geffen. Ultimately, though, Leo was thought to be too young. The role went to Christian Slater, giving Leo the chance to do an odd twenty-seven-minute film, *The Foot Shooting Party*.

Why not? In it Leo would play a young rocker who tries to escape being drafted and having to go to Vietnam. It's the early seventies, and the character intends to get out of the service by shooting himself in the foot. He realizes, however, that pulling the trigger is not that simple. The movie was executive-produced by Renny Harlin, best known for action-adventure films such as *Cliffhanger*, with Sylvester Stallone, and *Die Hard 2*, starring Bruce Willis.

Leo loved doing the film. It not only gave him a chance to "stretch his acting muscles," in a short, more experimental format, but to dress up in the hippie style his father used to wear. To achieve the long-haired look that was also needed to re-create the era, Leo had hair extensions added to his own blond locks. (This would not be the last time Leo could toss his hair around like Madonna, as he would also feature a great mane in *The Man in the Iron Mask*.)

Although few people ever saw *The Foot Shooting Party*, Leo regards it as a learning process. It wasn't long after Leonardo brandished a gun in *The Foot Shooting Party*,  that he would be slinging one in his next movie, *The Quick and the Dead*. Leonardo, however, wasn't originally keen on doing the movie, and turned it down. He gave it more thought, however, and decided not to pass up the chance to work with director Sam Raimi and costar Sharon Stone.

Stone was also one of the producers. It turns out that she wanted Leonardo in her film so badly that she personally came up with some of the money to pay his salary.

This fact added to the rumors that would swirl around the production that said the pair was having an affair during shooting. Because there was a romance scene—they wake up in bed together—the press had a field day. Sharon and Leonardo's comments put a quick end to the speculation, however.

Janet Maslin of *The New York Times* found Leonardo beguiling. "Commanding enough limelight to show why the camera loves him, [Leonardo DiCaprio] is immensely promising. And a brash, scrawny adolescent who is nick-named 'The Kid' can make even the most glamorous movie queen look like his mother."

Anthony Lane of *The New Yorker* also found gold in Leo's performance. "DiCaprio is well on his way to the held-back cockiness of the young Jack Nicholson, and it's hard to see how he can veer away from stardom now."

Leo's zooming star aside, the film did poorly at the box office, grossing only $20 million on a budget of $32 million. *The Quick and the Dead* has become somewhat of a cult film on video, though, and Leonardo's engaging performance as a brash, gun-toting kid is worth the watch. And hey, the kid even got pretty good at twirling that gun!

Although Leonardo's first venture into mainstream Hollywood was not a mega-success, Leonardo's bank account was growing. The little boy from the wrong part of Hollywood was having some real financial success. He was getting comfortable with this fact, and he began to enjoy spending some of his earnings, in spite of his reputation for being frugal.

Leo took great pride in the fact that he was able to surprise his father, George, with a car for his fiftieth birthday.

He orchestrated a big birthday bash for him with all of George's friends. Just as George was blowing out the candles on the cake Leo drove up and beeped in a brand-new car. George's face lit up!

And how. It was a great night and everyone had a fantastic time. Leo partied hard at the bash he threw for his father—dancing, doing his funny impressions, joking, and being his lovable self.

Not long after, when I was doing an article for a local newspaper for Father's Day, I asked Leo what advice his father had given him. He called me from his Jeep Cherokee and, though the phone kept cutting in and out, he was, as ever, completely honest... and adorable.

"Victoria," he said, "my father told me to never let anyone convince you that you know who you are as a human

Leo presents his father with quite a birthday gift

being... because you don't know who you are. You're always changing and finding new things. Don't get comfortable," Leo added, "in one way of being."

Wow! Leonardo as existentialist. The kid no doubt had it. Indeed, Leo was at the height of his career, moving from film to film, gaining stature, respect, and glowing reviews on the Hollywood circuit, yet he still retained his home-grown, earnest values. He was not letting fame go to his blond, teenaged head. He still enjoyed hanging out with friends and doing everyday things.

Soon it was time to decide what movie he would make next. Leo understood that he needed to be careful with his choices, as he was definitely on the fast track now. It would be in his best interest, then, to keep the momentum going. His next film would prove to be a radical departure. He opted to play drug-addicted poet Jim Carroll in *The Basketball Diaries.*

Based on the critically acclaimed memoirs of Jim Carroll's teen years as a Catholic high school basketball star, it is a vivid depiction of how Jim and his friends blew out of control into the scary world of drugs and crime. The book, first published in 1978, turned Carroll into a media darling, but it would still be fifteen years before it saw life as a film.

Indeed, many of Hollywood's hot young actors had wanted the role, even River Phoenix, who supposedly carried a copy of *The Basketball Diaries* around with him in his pocket. But Matt Dillon, Eric Stoltz, and even Johnny Depp had to turn the reins over to Leonardo, who was fascinated with the raw, honest script from the start. He also saw a chance to get an antidrug message across.

Leonardo developed the character of Jim with the help of a drug counselor whom he interviewed as part of his research, not by taking drugs himself. What may have looked like heroin in the movie was, in fact, Ovaltine. In any case, Leo was much too savvy to let a movie role become reality. He was certainly not about to step into River Phoenix's shoes, metaphorically or otherwise.

To imagine Leonardo shooting up is unfathomable. He has had a phobia of needles since he was a baby. George recalls, "When Leonardo was growing up I would take him to Dr. Fleiss [Paul Fleiss, the father of Hollywood Madam Heidi] for routine immunizations. We would be in the examining room waiting for the doctor, and Leonardo would say, 'Now, Daddy, you promised there wouldn't be any needles. You know I hate them.' I would say, 'No, no, Leonardo. The nurse is going to give you a pill instead.'

"Then the nurse would walk in with her tray, and a needle would be lying under some gauze. Leonardo would bolt up: 'Daddy, I see a needle there. I think we'd better go outside in the car to discuss this matter.' So I would take Leonardo out and we'd get into the car. 'Drive,' Leonardo would command. And this would be very funny, because we lived directly across the street from the doctor's office!"

Scott Kalvert had been hired to direct *The Basketball Diaries,* and it was his first feature. Kalvert's previous experience was directing MTV videos, several starring Marky Mark, who was ultimately cast in the film, but using his real name, Mark Wahlberg.

With Kalvert in place as director and Leo as Jim, Kalvert then cast Lorraine Bracco as Jim's mother, and James Madio and Patrick McGaw, who rounded out Jim's circle of hoop-shooting addict friends.

When filming began, Leonardo quickly immersed himself

in the role, as well as in New York City's night life. He relished the change between Los Angeles and the Big Apple, a city to which he would return time and again. Among other things, Leo loves New Yorkers' honesty. The shoot lasted eight weeks, with Kalvert and crew providing the requisite dirty abandoned buildings and seamy alleys as backdrops to the action. Shooting in New York can be chaotic, but real.

How real was subject for the gossip columnists. Leonardo soon became a regular item in all of the papers, allegedly clubbing and picking fights throughout the eternally electric New York nights, a modus operandi he would continue into the late nineties. Even back then, Leo's short list of dates read like a who's who of supermodels.

Leonardo always maintained that these nights partying were highly exaggerated and blown out of proportion. He refuses to stay cooped up in a hotel room to this day.

The printed accounts of Leonardo getting into knock-down drag-out fights, as it were, also called attention to the golden boy. The *New York Post* wrote: "DiCaprio hits Manhattan clubs and brawls with locals."

While putting in long, long days on the set, it was unlikely Leo would indulge his nights with fisticuffs. But his attitude, as always, remained on an even keel. He shrugged off the tabloids with comments about how scandal and gossip—not the truth—sell newspapers.

The Basketball Diaries was the first feature film that carried the name Leonardo DiCaprio above the title, proving that here was an actor who had the ability and star power to carry the weight of a film. After portraying a number of "troubled young man" characters, Leo brought all of his astonishing capabilities together to bring Jim Carroll to life, however seedy, sad, and lowdown his life may have been.

With the release of *The Basketball Diaries,* critics again couldn't stop talking about young Leo's gritty, realistic portrayal. *People* magazine wrote, "Leonardo DiCaprio proves yet again that he's the most promising actor around. DiCaprio's performance is flawless." *Rolling Stone*'s Peter Travers shouted, "Electrifying! A bust-out star performance!" And *The New York Times*' Janet Maslin touted, "DiCaprio is a latter-day James Dean."

All of this praise and adulation for young Leo ultimately could not save the film. *The Basketball Diaries* flickered briefly in the theaters before its flame was extinguished. The subject matter was thought, in the end, to be too dark for audiences.

Being compared to James Dean, though, sparked a renewed interest in Leo to play one of his screen heroes. After all, Leo was the kid who loved to go up to the observatory in Griffith Park and contemplate his future while gazing upon the bust of James Dean, who died in 1955 after making only three films. It was there that scenes had been filmed from *Rebel Without a Cause*.

In fact, Leo and I spent many an afternoon there, talking about the films of Dean and his life. Now Warner Bros. was planning to mount a lavish production about James Dean.

And Leonardo was their first choice.

Leo, after some hard thinking, decided against playing the young actor. The role called for a mere duplication of Dean, something Leo wasn't at all comfortable with.

His next decision surprised a lot of people. Leo would breathe life into the nineteenth-century French poet Arthur Rimbaud. *Total Eclipse* would give Leo the chance to explore another emotionally charged person, but it would bring the worst notices of his career.

The James Dean bust at Griffith Park Observatory

Next Leonardo briefly considered playing icon Jack Kerouac, whose book *On the Road* was in the hands of *Godfather* director

Francis Ford Coppola. I personally knew Jan Kerouac, the writer's only child who has since died, and during one of our visits in Marin County, she expressed a keen interest in Leonardo portraying her hard-living father.

Kerouac believed young Leonardo had the "edgy fearless-ness" of her father and a kind of "untamed brilliance" that would have come across on-screen. But Leo as road poet was not to be.

Strange Bedfellows: From Rimbaud to Romeo

Leonardo, at the ripe old age of twenty, was rich and famous. He had been working virtually nonstop for a third of his young life. The trajectory would continue, but not without grist for the gossip mills and the fickle public, who would have a difficult time accepting Leo as an absinthe-minded man in love with another man in nineteenth-century France.

In deciding to portray the life of Arthur Rimbaud, the hard-living homosexual poet who died at the age of thirty-seven in 1891, Leo took a gamble. He believed at the time that it would be one of the most important roles of his career. Besides, Leonardo really dug the character.

Thus did Leonardo fly to France to work with the director Agnieszka Holland, with a script written by Christopher Hampton. Hampton had written the film *Dangerous Liaisons,* another costume drama that starred John Malkovich and Keanu Reeves, and had been trying to bring *Total Eclipse* to the big screen since he had written it as a play while a student at Oxford in 1967.

Hampton's first choice for Rimbaud was none other than River Phoenix, who had agreed to do the film several years back. John Malkovich was slated to play poet Paul Verlaine, Rimbaud's lover and mentor. When Phoenix died, the part was up for grabs, but at that point, Malkovich lost interest in the project.

The door was now open for Leo. Hampton felt that the young dreamboat actually resembled Rimbaud. With Leonardo cast, the question then remained: Who would play Verlaine?

Holland, who had directed the film *Europa, Europa,* sought out the British actor David Thewlis, whose mesmerizing work in the Mike Leigh movie *Naked* had set tongues wagging several years back.

Leonardo, as it turns out, was positively ecstatic in being able to work with Thewlis. He and his friends were huge fans of *Naked*.

Although Leo was thrilled with the casting, he still had his reservations about several scenes in the movie, most notably those depicting sex. Initially Leo had been hesitant about doing the film—and his agent had certainly advised against him doing it—because of the rather graphic sex scenes between the poet lovers.

There had been earlier rumors about Leonardo's sexuality after the innocent kiss in *This Boy's Life,* and there had certainly been talk about some of the all-boy scenes in *The Basketball Diaries.* As it happens, the boy-oriented scenes in *This Boy's Life* and *The Basketball Diaries* were to pale in comparison to the blatant homosexual scenes in *Total Eclipse.* The movie was, after all, about the relationship between the two men, physical and otherwise.

Leo was adamant that the film was not about homosexuality, maintaining that it was about a young man who sought to experience everything life had to offer.

The other parallel with *The Basketball Diaries* was that its protagonists consumed large quantities of drugs. *Total Eclipse,* however, dealt with absinthe, an addictive type of wood grain alcohol made from the wormwood tree, not heroin, the twentieth-century drug of destruction that was the centerpiece of *The Basketball Diaries.* Another parallel is that both films delve into the lives of young writers. To re-create on-screen someone as bohemian as Rimbaud was part of the role's allure for the young actor.

Although Leonardo has never been a Method actor, his immersion into the role of Rimbaud got him writing poetry—again. Yes! Leonardo has always had a poetic and romantic streak, and had actually been jotting down some of his thoughts while making movies over the years. In fact, some of his poems can be found on the Internet.

Leo did admit, though, to being uncomfortable with the sex scenes. As before, he relaxed on the set—and got the cast and crew laughing—by joking.

Leo's lighter side always comes through

LEONARDO

Leonardo wasn't concerned that there would be a fan backlash to the portrayed homosexuality. He was rational about his new role and felt the project was risky, but intelligent.

Leo's mother, Irmelin, was on location in France during most of the filming of *Total Eclipse* and was even featured as an extra in the movie. She was one of the nurses who watched as the dying Rimbaud has his leg amputated after developing a tumor on his knee.

This certainly rang a bell for Leo: Irmelin's father, Leo's grandfather, was suffering from blood clots in his feet at the time and was to have his leg amputated. The surgery was postponed, but the ailing man died in late 1995, making it a particularly strenuous time for Leonardo. To top things off, Leo's beloved rottweiler, Rocky, had to be put down.

The film, for all of Leo's good intentions, flopped. In its first United States run it grossed only around $350,000, although it has gone on to become a cult hit on video. *Total Eclipse* was not a hit with the critics, either. Leonardo received the worst notices of his career. One particularly blistering review, which came out in *Screen International,* said: "As portrayed by Leonardo DiCaprio, in a potentially career-damaging performance, Rimbaud is a feral savant, suicidally uninhibited, endlessly annoying."

Leo, as ever, had his own feelings about *Total Eclipse,* as well as the unfavorable reviews. He remains proud of his work and the film's place in his body of work.

Leonardo believed in himself and his ability to choose intelligent, challenging film roles. If he had risked something, so be it, but his integrity was still intact. He would always come to the defense of his decisions, even if he did not necessarily understand the public's reactions.

With two films behind him that were not commercial successes, it might have seemed that Leonardo DiCaprio was entering a slump, that his star power was fading. He had been working steadily for many years and was, to put it bluntly, exhausted. Perhaps he needed to go home, chill out, relax with friends and family, because his next choice of roles would be crucial.

No one, however, would have expected the blond boy to attempt the classics. But with Leo, surprise is sometimes his middle name. Within a year, Leonardo DiCaprio would bring *William Shakespeare's Romeo & Juliet* to the screen in a way the world had never seen before. Leo would cause hearts to flutter and girls to weep with his portrayal of a twentieth-century Romeo. Talk about sheer charisma!

Leo certainly has it, but it was more on the urging of his father, George, that Leo accepted the project. George had been guiding Leonardo through the maze of Hollywood since his son's career began. Initially, Leo was not inclined to even give the script a second reading, but George had a

gut feeling about this film, and since Leonardo has always trusted and respected his father's instincts, the young actor gave it a shot.

Shakespeare beckoned. After all, many great thespians have done the Bard justice—from Sir Laurence Olivier and Al Pacino to Kenneth Branagh and Mel Gibson. But their versions, all wonderful, were not what Australian director Baz Luhrmann had in mind for his revisionist treatment of literature's most famous star-crossed lovers.

Luhrmann, who'd had a hit film with *Strictly Ballroom,* possessed a unique vision that would set fire to the screen—if only his Romeo were the perfect combination of young hormones raging in a blend of sizzle and sensuality.

Leo was certain he didn't want to do a traditional version of *Romeo & Juliet*. But here was a unique treatment as envisioned by Baz Luhrmann.

So George and Leonardo flew to Australia, where they would discover the limitless horizon of Luhrmann's imagination. It began with Leonardo doing a workshop with Luhrmann, and it ended up being a two-week stay that cemented a most fortuitous collaboration.

Persuading American studios to go for this updated classic was another story, but Luhrmann understood that Leonardo's casting would be the deciding factor. Luhrmann wisely videotaped the acting workshop he had done with Leo, using the footage to convince 20th Century Fox that his version of the classic tale would indeed draw in a young and potentially mass audience. With Leonardo on board, the production seemed to make more sense to the studios.

Leo and George, best buddies

Still, Leo felt slightly intimidated at the idea of actually reciting Shakespeare, and the idea of burrowing into a character so well known as Romeo—no matter that he is fictional—also proved challenging. Leo and Baz worked together and ultimately made the language sing.

Leonardo, suited up for the challenge, committed himself to the project with his typical 110 percent dynamism. With Leonardo in place, then, as the latter-day Romeo, Luhrmann mounted a massive search for his perfect Juliet. It seemed that every young actress—from Alicia Silverstone to Natalie Portman—auditioned for the part. And poor Leonardo! He had to play the same scene with each and every one of the aspirants.

The process seemed to drag on interminably. From the beginning, though, Leonardo had a sixth sense about Claire Danes. The actress first gained attention on television in *My So-Called Life,* before swiftly making the transition into films with *Little Women.* Leo was already a fan. When Claire came in and read, both star and director knew the long search had ended. Claire's reading was forceful and convincing. Luhrmann knew he had the perfect pairing of on-screen chemistry between two fantastic actors.

The film was shot over three months' time in and around Mexico City. From the vast and barren lands of Texcoco to the renowned Chapultepec Castle, and the beaches of Veracruz, Luhrmann created a mythical world that would be known to the moviegoing public as Verona Beach, U.S.A. Think: a little Miami Beach, a little madness, and a lot of make-believe mayhem!

Indeed, some of that mayhem proved real, as the shoot was not without problems. Among them was a ninety-mile-per-hour sandstorm that blew up, halting filming on the beach and toppling standing sets. This was followed by a series of attacks from killer bees and even a bout with food poisoning, which halted production for four days. Both cast and crew experienced dysentery.

In spite of the production problems, Luhrmann stayed on track and was true to Shakespeare's text and basic scene structure: The audience first meets the Montague and Capulet gangs, with Tybalt on the Capulets' side and Mercutio on the Montagues' side; Romeo spots Juliet— here it is through the glass of an aquarium at the Capulets' masked ball—and then it's love at first sight.

Instead of swords, as previously mentioned, the universe of Romeo and Juliet is one of hot-rod cars, helicopters, and designer guns. It is also one photographed in brilliant colors, particularly the lustrous primaries of yellows and blues as well as tangerines and mystical purples.

Contemporizing the film further, Luhrmann adds to the famous balcony scene, with the doomed lovers exchanging their vows in a brilliant turquoise swimming pool.

The actors, whatever doubts they may have initially harbored, did a splendid job, certainly one on a par with Luhrmann's sumptuous vision. The result: a bountiful feast for the eyes, layered with the immortal words of William Shakespeare.

Pushing the envelope as far as he could, the director also took liberties with his characterizations. Juliet's mother is a pill-popping alcoholic, the nurse is no less than a babbling busybody, and Harold Perrineau's Mercutio? He's a drug-taking drag queen at the ball.

Welcome to the MTV generation of William Shakespeare! Wanting to connect with a postmodern nineties audience, Luhrmann succeeded in a way that actually made Elizabethan language hip. The director brought all of his disparate elements together with exceptional panache. His Romeo was a chain smoker who recited poetry, a true romantic hero for the turn of the millennium. And it took someone like Leonardo to pull it off.

The fruits of Leo's labors were definitely adding up on-screen. Off-screen, however, Leo found that he really needed to let off some steam. After gaining a reputation as a party guy while shooting *The Basketball Diaries,* Leo carried on the tradition in Mexico. When the actors were not filming, they were often found horsing around or carry-ing on in the hotel swimming pool, as well as videotaping their hotel room parties.

Leo shopping for *Romeo & Juliet* souvenirs

Partying with his fellow actors was fun, but Leo also liked to be surrounded with good friends. The young star had a clause in his contract that allowed him to fly his buddies down to film shoots. Several of his pals had flown in from New York, and one night Leonardo and posse, along with Claire, decided to go to a nightclub. What started as a simple night out quickly escalated into unabashed lunacy. The bouncer at the club picked a fight with one of Leo's friends, which eventually turned into a brawl and several broken ribs for Leo's buddy.

It's not that the production was cursed, but strange things seemed to be happening everywhere, as if Shakespeare himself had dreamed up a strange brew. That same night a crew member was hospitalized after a taxi he was riding in was hijacked by a trio of men who slammed his head against the pavement and issued death threats if they weren't given the whopping sum of four hundred dollars.

Leonardo commented, "It must have been a full moon."

The full moon was not accountable for Leonardo's on-set antics and impersonations, however. In order to stave off boredom between takes, he would do a killer Michael Jackson, and when he finished with that, Leo would imitate the rest of the cast with their Shakespearean line deliveries.

Even Claire, who prides herself in being a serious actress, accepted Leo's practical jokes, along with his friends' antics, and gave in to the fact that her Romeo and his posse were nothing but clowns. They began a wonderful friendship, too.

But did she fall in love with Leo off-screen? Claire doesn't mince words. "We really clicked. It's great when you find someone who you understand." The pair may have indulged in steamy love scenes on-screen, but that was the extent of it.

Leonardo realized that he had a lot of admirers in Mexico, with girls seeking him out just to get a look at his famous face. From nightclubbing to turning in a masterful performance as a full-blown heartthrob, Leonardo DiCaprio's international image was cemented. In his first on-screen hero portrayal, Leo got to the core of the character that has remained essentially timeless. It paid off big-time.

When the film was released, it soared to number one at the box office. It took in $36 million in its first month of release, soon passing the $50 million mark.

No small potatoes for a film that was shot in seventy-two days and had a $15 million budget. Again, Leo's work was cited for its originality and depth. *Sight and Sound* said, "[Leonardo, as Romeo] is the one who bears the brunt of feeling: It's his face in close-up most of the time indicating how he wants, longs, feels and sometimes, eyes hidden by tears, suffers. His performance is all raw emotion.... It's a superb performance."

The soundtrack, too, proved to be a hit with young audiences. In fact, there were two separate soundtracks from the film, one with the background music alone, the other with the rock groups The Cure, Nirvana, and Garbage, among others.

It was now official: Leonardo DiCaprio, famous for his troubled teen portrayals, had broken through to Hollywood's A list with his mesmerizing characterization of one of literature's most famous heroes. One no longer needed to ask the question "Romeo, Romeo, wherefore art thou?" Romeo was in your face, and in your heart, worldwide in one of the decade's most daring and audacious films.

And Leonardo DiCaprio was unquestionably at the film's center.

That first weekend, when *Romeo & Juliet* bowed at number one at the box office, Leonardo was celebrating his twenty-second birthday. Born November 11, Leonardo is a true Scorpio—sexy, powerful, kind-hearted, and even a bit whimsical. He was a major movie star, but he always had time for his friends and family.

Instead of having a big bash at a nightclub, as he'd done for his twenty-first birthday, he opted to party in one of his favorite spots, Griffith Park. He'd gone there so often as a child and truly loved being out in nature.

Today would be his day to celebrate and relax. His movie was a hit, but he was not about to rest on his laurels. After wrapping *Romeo & Juliet,* the actor had turned down the role of Dirk Diggler in *Boogie Nights,* leaving the door open for his friend, Mark Wahlberg, to play that role. Leo had, instead, decided to take the lead in the big-budget movie *Titanic,* directed by James Cameron. So again Leonardo found himself working in Mexico, this time in Rosarito Beach, on the Baja peninsula.

For now, though, Leo had temporarily left the part of free-spirited Jack Dawson behind him. He relaxed and had fun at Griffith Park and chowed down on pasta, fresh-baked breads, and salads, and even knocked back a few beers. He was surrounded by his favorite people. Instead of having to dress up in the period costumes of the early twentieth century, Leonardo could really be himself in baggy gym shorts, a tank T-shirt, and a floral headband.

The guys were running around the meadow playing touch football, with Leonardo doing plenty of legwork, both passing and catching. He probably was exacerbating an old knee injury, which would give him problems and require surgery in the near future, but for now, he just got off on the high energy and vibes of the beautiful day.

Besides some of his posse—Jonah Johnson, Toby Maguire, and Ethan Suplee—Baz Luhrmann was there, as was Leo's pediatrician, Dr. Paul Fleiss, father of Hollywood Madam Heidi. In fact, Dr. Fleiss is still Leo's doctor, and besides being a family friend, in true Hippocratic fashion, he had recently made several house calls to Leo, who had been exhausted from nonstop working.

Leo's girlfriend at the time, model Kristen Zang, was all smiles, watching Leo get tackled. In fact, I felt really cool when Leo introduced me to Kristen: "Victoria, yeah—she's the Juliet of Public Access."

I didn't quite know what he meant, but I dug it nonetheless.

As far as Hollywood parties go, this one seemed to have it all—though valet parking was definitely not needed! Even the world's most famous houseguest, Kato Kaelin, wandered in, though Leo refused to have his picture taken with him. One of Leo's favorite actors, Bud Cort, who had starred in the cult classic film *Harold and Maude,* also made an appearance.

Meanwhile, George and Peggy had strung up a large piñata from a tree and we all gathered around so Leonardo could attempt to knock it down. The wildest part? Leo was blindfolded. With lots of coaxing from the cheering crowd, Leo finally made a hit and the thing came tumbling to the ground, narrowly missing his now very famous blond head.

Among the gifts Leo received that day were a few pairs of heart-emblazoned Heidi Wear boxer shorts (compliments of his pediatrician), a monogrammed Hollywood Star Lanes bowling shirt, a Chicago Bulls jersey, and a new supply of my music tapes, *Harpnosis,* that he could use for relaxation while on difficult film shoots.

As the sun began to set, Leo blew out the candles on a huge birthday cake. His wish, no doubt, had already come true, but soon enough his star would move into the stratosphere far beyond his wildest dreams.

In true Hollywood fashion, Leonardo DiCaprio would be riding the crest of one of the hugest popularity waves in cinematic history. For now, though, he was just Leo— laughing, joking, hanging out with the people who mattered most to him, and loving, oh, yeah, loving...and feasting upon life.

CHAPTER SEVEN

Leonardo's Room...and Reputation

Back in 1992, when Leonardo was on my TV show, *The Looseleaf Report,* he didn't want to discuss the possibility of making the film adaptation of *Marvin's Room,* for fear of "jinxing" the project. By the end of 1996, however, the film was not only in the can, it was being released as a Christmas movie.

The casting of Leonardo as Hank, another troubled teen whose family is in the midst of a crisis, was largely due to Leo's old pal, Bobby De Niro, who not only acted in the film, but was one of its producers. *Marvin's Room,* incidentally, won the Golden St. George grand prize for Best Picture at the Moscow International Film Festival. De Niro flew to Russia to accept the award in July of 1997, while Leonardo was busy looping *Titanic.*

Before Leo decided to commit to *Marvin's Room,* many of his handlers and advisers staunchly believed he was ready for more adult roles. Leo, too, was looking forward to playing parts closer to his age, but the youthful star wasn't about to pass up the opportunity to work with some of Hollywood's most prestigious actors.

He defended his decision to perform on-screen as another disaffected youth. After all, he would never be able to play teenage roles again. For now, his baby-face looks belied his chronological age and maturity.

The biggest drawing card of *Marvin's Room* for the young actor was the company he would be keeping. Besides De Niro, Leo would be acting with Meryl Streep and Diane Keaton, who would go on to win an Oscar nomination for her stirring performance as the ailing Bessie.

Based on a hit off-Broadway play by Scott McPherson, *Marvin's Room* is the story of two sisters, Lee and Bessie, played by Streep and Keaton. Lee, who had been the inde-

pendent, butterfly-
spirited sibling,
had left home
years ago in search
of a more exotic
life, while Bessie
stayed home to
care for the sisters'
bedridden father.

When Lee's rebel-
lious son Hank
burns down their
home, she packs
their bags, and,
along with brother
Charlie (played by Hal Scardino), the family heads to Florida
and Bessie. It is at this time that Bessie is stricken with
leukemia and, instead of being the caregiver, now needs to
be taken care of herself. It would be the first time Lee's
family meets Aunt Bessie and Grandpa Marvin, played by
the incomparable stage actor, Hume Cronyn. De Niro plays
the compassionate Dr. Wally, who treats Bessie, and Gwen
Verdon plays Marvin's sister, the eccentric Aunt Ruth.

In essence, this is another dysfunctional family in need
of healing.

Leo had first read the script while he was making *This*

Boy's Life. Although the family dynamics were nothing like his own, the youth was so impressed by what he'd read that he told De Niro he wanted to be a part of it.

It is certainly a measure of Leo's taste and ability to choose worthy projects at such a young age that he was able to discern the value of a script like *Marvin's Room.* His not wishing to discuss it on my TV show for fear of putting the kibosh on it only underscored his desire to do the picture.

When the green light was given to *Marvin's Room,* theater director Jerry Zaks was slated to helm the top-notch cast. Among the actors there had already been nineteen Oscar nominations and five wins. Leonardo would certainly fit in, having garnered one nomination himself, for his role of Arnie in *What's Eating Gilbert Grape?* And although Hank was yet another troubled teen with mental health problems, this was more an opportunity for Leonardo to flex his acting muscles in a slightly different direction.

Leonardo adored working with this brilliant ensemble cast, as they did with him. Leo had a number of scenes with Keaton's Aunt Bessie, who loves him unconditionally. Keaton, as it turns out, was also completely enamored with the young actor off the set as well. She spoke glowingly of his talents and sense of humor. While Leo had a great time working with Keaton, he also, true to himself, enjoyed being mischievous with her.

While Leonardo was the object of Keaton's affection, the young star also won over Meryl Streep. Leo dug Streep's work and admired the actress herself. Their work together in *Marvin's Room* was intense and compelling.

Leonardo was leading a charmed life. Affirming his stature as a Hollywood player, his daily routines were beginning to fuel people's curiosity. Leonardo at this time began getting more press coverage than he had previously. Fans had been getting to know his on-screen persona; now they wanted to know about his private life: Where did he go? Who were his friends? What was he really like?

Of course, there was much speculation as to Leonardo's romantic life. He had been tied to a number of female friends from Sara Gilbert and Juliette Lewis to Alicia Silverstone and Demi Moore. While Leo's friendship with Alicia was due to the fact that they had had nearly parallel careers and had both taken a self-help course, The Forum, nothing really came of their acquaintance.

Sure, Alicia had told an interviewer she thought "Leo is pretty cool," but this is a sentiment most of the world shares.

As for Sara Gilbert, who had been on the hit show *Roseanne,* she had invited Leonardo to be her date for her boss's wedding to Tom Arnold. Leo accepted—as a friend—but the high point of that evening was not a romantic tryst for the burgeoning hunk, but watching Roseanne eat her multitiered wedding cake.

While the rumor mills churned out endless pairings between Leo and his various costars, such as Claire Danes and, later, *Titanic*'s Kate Winslet, Leonardo is a firm believer in not mixing so-called business with pleasure. Nevertheless, the tabloid frenzy began and it would be part and parcel of Leonardo's life as one of the biggest movie stars in the world.

How the tabloids picked up and ran with a story that claimed Leonardo was having an affair with Demi Moore, mother of three and wife of superstar Bruce Willis, is an example of the public's overt hunger for any tidbit of gossip surrounding Hollywood players.

The pair, as the world soon discovered, were merely friends, enjoying a harmless night of coffee, pizza, and conversation. Demi Moore was developing a film project that dealt with an older woman/younger man relationship. She and Leo had a meeting to discuss this—simply business. This statement was released to *News of the World*: "Demi wanted to meet Leonardo to see if they had any chemistry together."

Leonardo did not allow himself to get flustered. He constantly reiterated that he and Demi were merely friends.

What really quashed the rumor of the Moore/DiCaprio romance, however, was the fact that Leonardo actually had a girlfriend at this time, model Kristen Zang. Leonardo, as his star—and star power—rose, had gradually begun shedding his T-shirt and lumber jacket image, the one I had known him to sport for so many years, in favor of a more high fashion look. He also began attending fashion shows, which is where he met Zang. He later took her to the premier of *Romeo & Juliet*.

Even though Leonardo would fly Kristen down to Mexico to visit him on location during the filming of *Titanic*, the pair, after going together for about fifteen months, ultimately broke up. Leo seems to be in no big rush to settle down. No doubt he's aware of the relationship his father, George, had with his wife, Peggy. The pair did in fact live together for nearly two decades before officially tying the knot, which took place at the home of Dr. Timothy Leary on Valentine's Day in 1996. Leary, who died shortly thereafter from cancer, was best known as the Harvard psychologist who experimented with the psychedelic drug, LSD. His death became a worldwide event through postings on the Internet and much media attention, climaxing in Leary's ashes being shot into outer space.

George and Peggy's unconventional relationship, which culminated in a most unconventional wedding, with Leo very much in attendance, no doubt gave Leo food for thought about his own life.

It was work, not love, that seemed to dominate Leo's life at this point, along with a bit of daredevilry. Always eager to explore his adventurous side, Leonardo narrowly escaped a catastrophe while sowing his wild oats in his first attempt at skydiving. He was celebrating his friend Justin Herwick's twenty-first birthday by taking to the air.

There they were, along with instructor Harley Powell, 12,500 feet above the Mojave Desert when Leonardo, after jumping from the plane, tugged on his rip cord... and nothing happened. Leo continued falling for about twenty seconds, until Powell managed to get Leonardo to pull his emergency backup parachute cord. Leo floated to the ground, thankfully none the worse for wear.

Leo may have nixed further skydiving exploits, but the hair-raising experience did not prevent him from making a brief foray into bungee jumping. Alas, even bungee jumping didn't do it for the kid who was soon to be on top of the world, so Leo followed that with off-road vehicle racing while filming *The Man in the Iron Mask*.

Wow! Leo had certainly come a long way from bicycle riding in Concrete, Washington, to zooming around quaint country roads in France. Ultimately, however, it was the work he would do in James Cameron's epic film *Titanic* that would inextricably change Leonardo DiCaprio forever.

King of the World

More words have been written about the sinking of the *Titanic*, it seems, than on any other catastrophe in modern history. And more words have been written about *Titanic*, the Oscar-winning James Cameron epic, than nearly any other cinematic effort to date. What is its ongoing allure, the hold the ill-fated ship has on its public? What really happened that night of April 14, 1912? What might have happened to some of the ship's passengers? What would be the definitive and last word on the subject?

All of these questions have been broached over the years, but perhaps no answers have come together so brilliantly, so originally, and so successfully as they have in James Cameron's singular vision, the 1997 blockbuster film *Titanic*.

Even more to the point: With the charismatic Leonardo DiCaprio starring as the poor doomed artist who falls in love with a first-class passenger, the moviegoing public would become fascinated to the point of mania with a colossally bright, shining star.

Leonardo DiCaprio, at age twenty-three, is now "King of the World"!

To call director James Cameron obsessive is an apt description that readily comes to mind when one ponders his legendary film. The fact is, Cameron's interest in the *Titanic,* the ship, bordered on fanatic. But his reputation as a big-budget action director preceded him, so by the time *Titanic,* the film, became a reality, the pieces had already fallen somewhat neatly into place.

Cameron's 1985 *Terminator* film, starring Arnold Schwarzenegger, came in on budget at $18 million, a figure that seems ridiculously low by today's standards. Following that hit were *Aliens* and *Terminator 2,* which at $93 million was upping the production ante. Cameron then bettered himself with *True Lies,* which cost a then-whopping $100 million. In between Cameron suffered a critical and box office flop with his aquatic adventure, *The Abyss.*

But his desire to return to the sea was overwhelming.

Cameron was adamant about bringing his *Titanic* passion to life. Yes, the story of the ill-fated ship was just too good to be left at the bottom of the sea. Built between 1910 and 1912 at a staggering cost of $7.3 million, the *Titanic* was unequivocally the most lavish ship of its era. As nearly everyone now knows—from cinema buff to history fanatic—the good ship sank on April 14, 1912, five days into its maiden voyage from Southampton to New York.

Indeed. It had done the inconceivable: Four hundred miles off the coast of Newfoundland, *Titanic* hit an iceberg. Nearly 1,600 people died, with 700 or so surviving. In the ensuing years, the tragedy of *Titanic* was the germ for an array of films, documentaries, books, CD-ROMs, CDs, TV miniseries, and even a hit Broadway musical.

Yes, the *Titanic* may have sunk, but its tale absolutely refuses to die. The 1953 film was a black-and-white feature starring Barbara Stanwyck and Clifton Webb playing out the tragedy. Lord Lew Grade produced a seventies version, *Raise the Titanic,* which ultimately proved more disastrous than its premise.

But nothing could come close to James Cameron's vision. The definitive epic—it clocks in at three hours and fourteen minutes—would ultimately cost the record-busting price of $200 million. It would, however, put to rest any future *Titanic* cinematic renderings. Produced as a joint effort by two studios, 20th Century Fox and Paramount, the last word on *Titanic* would be Cameron's.

Cameron would not only produce and direct the film, he would script it as well. He had decided to book-end his story, which would be told in flashback, by footage of the actual wreckage of the *Titanic*. Filmed by an underwater camera crew at the towering price of $4.5 million, this was merely the beginning. Cameron, in true auteur style, opted to build a nearly life-size model of the doomed ship as opposed to working with scale models and special effects. Which isn't to say that there wouldn't be special effects galore.

Cameron's boat measured nearly 800 feet in length, about as huge as the *Titanic* itself. It would be docked in Rosarito Beach, Mexico, the film's location, where Fox had constructed a mini-movie studio, replete with three sound stages and production offices.

The tank where the set was built held millions of gallons of water and no detail was spared—from re-creating the ship's china to authenticating its wood paneling. (While certain naysayers chided Cameron for featuring replicas of Picasso masterworks that obviously never made that voyage, this kind of detail apparently was overlooked or did not faze the director.)

To stage the actual sinking of the ship, tremendous hydraulic pistons abutted the entire construction. This special effect, as so oftentimes happens with men, machines, and movies, would result in injuries for some of the cast and crew.

In any case, the director now had his boat, his location, and the go-ahead for his baby. Now all James Cameron needed was the perfect cast.

Whoever would have dreamed it would be young Leo DiCaprio, now twenty-one, but still able to pass for seventeen? Leo had proven himself in an assortment of misfit, tortured teen roles, yes, and had, absolutely confirmed his leading man status in the runaway hit *Romeo & Juliet*. But assuming the mantle of romantic hero in the most expensive Hollywood movie ever made?

Jim Cameron considered a number of other young, hot actors. But when he met Leo he was convinced. In spite of Leonardo's A-list status, the star was still required to audition for the role of the passionate artist.

Leonardo, on the other hand, was not entirely convinced that he wanted to undertake a big Hollywood production. He had, after all, been offered the role of a seventies porn star, Dirk Diggler in *Boogie Nights*. But the challenge of playing the hero, artist Jack Dawson—and receiving his first paycheck for over $1 million—proved too great an enticement.

Leo admired Jack's happy, bohemian lifestyle and his big heart. He also liked the story, which Cameron had fashioned as a basic love duet. While Cameron's forte had been action—which this movie would certainly feature, in spades—Leo was concerned about the human scale. Was there a true heart to the movie? Oh, yes, there was!

Leo's love interest would be the appealing young British actress Kate Winslet, who had made a name for herself in such films as *Heavenly Creatures* and *Sense and Sensibility,* for which she was nominated for an Oscar.

Kate, who had already been a fan of Leo's before they met on the set of *Titanic,* had once confessed that she had wanted to play Juliet to his Romeo.

The opening scenes feature the before-mentioned footage of the real *Titanic,* followed by the introduction to one of the ship's living survivors, the fictional Rose, played by eighty-seven-year-old Gloria Stuart. Taken to see the ruins of the ship, Rose is overcome by waves of nostalgia; she is taken back to her past.

Cut to 1912 and the opulence of the *Titanic,* with Rose filling in the narrative, including her brief but blazing romance with Jack Dawson, who had won third-class passage for the catastrophic voyage in a card game. A simple story set against a monumental backdrop, *Titanic* also features a host of other characters.

Among them are Rose's mother, Ruth (Frances Fisher), who is trying to assure the marriage of her daughter to an exceedingly spoiled and very rich creep, Cal Hockley (Billy

Zane). Kathy Bates also makes a vivid Molly Brown.

The story is set in motion as Rose, unhappy with the prospect of an empty life, tries to kill herself by jumping off the back of the boat. It is here that she is rescued by that scruffy stranger, Jack Dawson. Their meeting immediately blurs class lines, providing, in a sense, a magnet for undying love. The classic love story.

While Leo had played period performances before (*Total Eclipse*), filming *Titanic* required him to also re-create the milieu of 1912—from manners, to dialect, to dancing. To accomplish this, dialect coach Susan Hegarty was hired to instruct the actors, both in behavior and speech, while Lynne Hockney was recruited as choreographer and etiquette coach. Most people on the set were shocked at Leo's excellent dancing.

I wouldn't have been shocked. I'd seen Leo break out in many an impromptu dance in the past—from Michael Jackson "moonwalking" to what looked like a kind of leaping pirouette from *Swan Lake*.

A controversial moment in the film is a scene where Rose prominently gives the finger to her fiancé's manservant. Definitely not a custom from 1912. Cameron had promised Kate that he would not use that take, as she had objected strenuously to its authenticity, but in the end Cameron, as auteur, ruled.

Another Cameron moment: The now-famous scene where

Jack is sketching Rose nude was to have ended with Jack, overcome by passion, bounding from his chair over to Rose. They would then make love for the first time on the sofa. Cameron filmed this scene, but it was not used in the final cut. Cameron opted to go for the couple entwined in an automobile in the ship's hold for their lovemaking debut.

There would ultimately be no arguing with the obsessed Cameron. Leonardo often found himself embroiled in debates about dialogue. He believed some of it to be unrealistic and would occasionally change wording as he saw fit.

While internal set-tos were common during the making of *Titanic,* the shoot also had its share of calamities, not unlike the vexing things that occurred in Mexico when Leo was filming *Romeo & Juliet.* Leo and most of the cast and crew were housed at the relatively posh Marriott Residence Inn Real Del Mar, about twenty minutes down the coast from the makeshift Fox Baja Studios.

There Leo could, ostensibly, refresh and regroup himself in the hotel's spa and sauna, also availing himself of therapeutic massages. Although pampering was in order, there was actually little time to partake in same, as one ordeal, it seemed, after another presented itself. But hey—this was the filming of *Titanic,* one of history's definitive disasters. Whether it was art imitating life or vice versa, calamities were fairly routine: actors and extras incurred broken ribs and sprained ankles during the shooting of the climactic sinking scenes. Crew members, too, required surgery after tumbling onto railings when the deck of the ship, while sinking, tilted at right angles.

Another case of art imitating life, or art imitating celluloid, was this: In the midst of shooting a storm scene, with Leo and Kate firmly tied to the ship's rail, a real storm whipped up.

After *Time* magazine reported at the end of 1996 that *Titanic* had indeed been the scene of many injuries, the Screen Actors Guild sent a representative to check on things. The guild found nothing running afoul of safety standards. One member of the production team noted, "Jim [Cameron] will put himself in danger before anyone else."

Leonardo spent six months filming *Titanic* in Mexico, not to mention his post-production looping and dubbing done later. His work weeks had been strenuous and long, occasionally lasting some seventy hours. But the young actor knew he had made the right choice and had an inkling that the film might really fly.

The magnitude of the movie was matched by the magnitude of Leonardo's gutsy, skillful performance. This truly was a Leonardo unlike any the world had seen before. And *Titanic* would be a film unlike any other. Cameron ultimately went $100 million over budget. *Titanic* was his baby and he was bound and determined to get it right according to his specifications and vision. The ship would, of course, sink, but everything else about the epic film would positively soar.

Titanic was originally slated for a July 4, 1997 release. As early as spring, Paramount Pictures was concerned that the movie would not make this date, suggesting instead that a November debut would be more likely.

While principal photography had been completed in March and digital effects were under way—Cameron's own company, Digital Domain, was initially responsible for the computerized effects—the budget had mushroomed to an all-time high of $200 million. *Titanic* would become the most expensive film of all time. And even if the film did well, it would still need to do about $500 million in business worldwide for either of the two studios involved to see profit. The 1996 blockbuster *Mission: Impossible,* which was deemed a worldwide success, had only grossed around $450 million globally.

No one entity was willing to take responsibility at this point. Were the delays Cameron's fault or was Digital Domain to blame? Cameron had begun to utilize the services of other effects houses, including those at Industrial Light and Magic. It seems that a panic resembling that exhibited on the *Titanic* itself was starting to spread among insiders.

When the official United States release date of December 19 was announced, a sigh of relief was breathed. A buzz—

this time positive—was beginning. Test audiences from cities as disparate as Minneapolis and Riverside, California, were reporting glowing reviews.

And then the tsunami hit.

Titanic would have its world premiere in Tokyo, on November 1, 1997, as the centerpiece of the Tokyo International Film Festival. Leonardo, along with director Cameron, was asked to make personal appearances. The world stood up and took notice as thousands of young Japanese girls began screaming, "Leo, Leo." Nothing had been seen on this scale since Beatlemania, more than thirty years ago.

Leo and Leomania had arrived. The golden boy who was about to turn twenty-three said to the adoring, screaming throngs of teenage girls, some of whom were in tears, "*Titanic* made a man out of me."

And a superstar! Even his bout with sampling fugu, Japanese blowfish, at the Okura Hotel would not deter his encroaching stardom. Fugu, which costs $500 a forkful, or $2,000 a portion, is not only one of the most expensive foods of the world, but it is potentially lethal. To be eaten, the fish must be in season and must be cut and served by a master sushi chef—one who has been trained for years—in order that the poisonous portion be removed.

Leo, clown that he is, evidently gave his posse a scare when he feigned choking after sampling a bite of the delicacy. The star, fortunately, was very much still alive!

Titanic opened number one at the box office in the States the week before Christmas, bringing in a reported $28.6 million. The sinking ship managed to keep the new James Bond movie, *Tomorrow Never Dies*, at bay and in second place, with its box-office gross of $26 million.

Titanic opened strong, yes, but it fell far short of the previous week's boffo hit, *Scream 2*, which managed to bring in about $33 million its opening weekend. And though the opening wasn't as huge as Paramount and Fox had hoped, the studios began to see gold the following week when the box office rose to $35.4 million, largely due to overwhelmingly positive reviews and even greater word of mouth.

Titanic had become the talk of the town, remaining at number one yet a third week...and a fourth...and yet again a fifth, until the boat that took a bath remained at number one for fifteen—count 'em—fifteen consecutive weeks. In fact, it remained in the top ten for a mind-boggling, record-breaking twenty-six weeks.

While much of the appeal lay in the film's special effects, the overriding factor had more to do with the love story. Even more so, with Leonardo as the riveting yet doomed hero. *Titanic* was being compared to, among other films, *Dr. Zhivago* and *Gone With the Wind*. Young Leo was being called a Clark Gable for his generation. Indeed, Olivia de Havilland, the lone surviving star of *Gone With the*

Wind, recently said of Leonardo in a *Los Angeles Times* interview: "I find him quite beguiling, fresh and likable. He's very young, a special type."

People magazine gushed over the chemistry between Leonardo and his costar, Kate Winslet, calling it "genuinely affecting." While the film's length may have at first been a turn-off to many people, it proved a draw for those who just couldn't get enough of young Leo's bravura dash and appeal. Film critic Lisa Schwarzbaum said, "When people talk about the magic of the movies, they mean this."

Entertainment Weekly cited *Titanic* as one of the top ten films of 1997, and *Titanic* sailed to the top of many a film reviewer's "best of" list. In fact, *Titanic's* numbers are so massive, one wonders if the records it keeps setting will ever end. The most popular movie of all time has roared past hype and hyperbole to become fact and now legend. In fact, the next edition of *The Guinness Book of World Records* is devoting a special section to the film.

Before the record books began calling, however, awards were in order. In January 1998, the annual Golden Globes, generally deemed a barometer for Oscar nominations, summoned *Titanic* front and center. The disaster movie racked up eight nominations.

James Cameron won Golden Globes for best picture and best director, while the film won for best score and for best song. Leonardo and Kate Winslet had both been nominated for best actor and actress respectively, but neither went home that night with statuettes. Peter Fonda won for *Ulee's Gold* and Dame Judi Dench was singled out for her performance in *Mrs. Brown*.

More important, however, were the Oscars themselves. Nominations were announced in February, with *Titanic* garnering a record number—fourteen. No other movie since 1950's *All About Eve* had received that many nominations. The most shocking surprise, however, was that Leonardo DiCaprio's name was not among the nominees. Kate Winslet was nominated for best actress, Gloria Stuart was nominated for best supporting actress, but, alas, no Leo.

The New York *Daily News* ran its February 11, 1998, headline as follows: "Oscar Sinks Hunk—14 nominations for *Titanic* tie Oscar record, but heartthrob Leonardo DiCaprio is snubbed."

Snubbed?

Leo had no comment. His father said to me, "What could he possibly say at this point? For him to say anything would be foolish. There's really nothing he can say."

Everyone else would do the talking. And most people were agreeing that Leo unfortunately came up against some very stiff competition: Matt Damon, Robert Duvall, Peter Fonda, Dustin Hoffman, and Jack Nicholson (who would ultimately bring home the gold for his obsessive-compulsive performance in *As Good As It Gets*).

Leo was both cavalier and stoical about his non-nomination. Remember, this was a guy who wasn't crazy about crowds or having to deliver speeches in front of an audience. The fact remains: Leo probably got more press by being shut out of the nominations than those who ultimately were part of the inner circle.

Leo chose not to go to Los Angeles' Shrine Auditorium the night of March 23, 1998, when the Oscars were awarded. Many people cited him as being a poor sport, but the truth is, he was out of town and preferred being out of the spotlight as well.

Besides, who could have topped James Cameron's acceptance speech when he won for best director? He called himself, in no less than titanic style, "King of the World."

Later, Cameron came back to the stage to collect the best picture statuette. He asked the audience to take "a few seconds of silence" to remember the *Titanic* dead, then suggested they "party till dawn." Frank Rich, in a subsequent *New York Times* column, reported that an industry observer had said, "In the first speech he was going for king. In the second he decided to go for God." Cameron's ego was not the ultimate crowd pleaser.

But celebrity rules. And who knows? Perhaps only God could have created a Leonardo DiCaprio, whose star is shining bigger and brighter than any other in the world in 1998.

CHAPTER NINE

Unsinkable, Unstoppable, Unpredictable: His Heart Will Go On

One would think that after wrapping the biggest budgeted flick in all of Hollywood history, Leonardo DiCaprio would take a breather —some time off. But no, Leo had previously signed on to play not one but two roles in a new version of the costume romp, *The Man in the Iron Mask*. Adapted from the Alexandre Dumas novel, it was to be directed by Randall Wallace, the Oscar-winning screenwriter for Mel Gibson's *Braveheart*.

Mask would give Leonardo a chance to work with screen icons John Malkovich, who had bowed out of *Total Eclipse,* Jeremy Irons, Gerard Depardieu, and Gabriel Byrne.

Leo would play the dual roles of King Louis and his evil twin brother. Although he would again be filming in France (the third time's the charm), he was at last much happier to be back on terra firma. The film was a departure of sorts. He was thrilled to be playing a villain.

Leo's contract had again stipulated he could bring some

Leo and George on location in France

of his buddies to France during portions of the shoot. His parents, too, arrived for a short visit with Leo.

Shooting *The Man in the Iron Mask* proved far easier than working on *Titanic,* as anything, no doubt, would be. Leo even had time to reignite his love for art and was almost able to enjoy an excursion to the Louvre. I say almost, because the youthful star discovered that he was not able to behold the Mona Lisa in peace: Hordes of young girls spotted Leo and began screaming before chasing him through the hallowed museum halls.

Leo was also staked out at his Champs Elysées apartment. And this, long before *Titanic* had docked into movie theaters the world over.

And who else but Leonardo DiCaprio could compete with Leonardo DiCaprio at the box office? The global star nearly knocked himself out of first place in the spring of 1998, when *The Man in the Iron Mask* debuted at the number two slot at the box office, second to—what else?—*Titanic.* Reviews, however, were not all that great, with even several in Leo's camp deriding the film.

No matter. *The Man in the Iron Mask* not only has proven to be another money-maker, with Leo's millions of fans flocking to see him in long hair and sumptuous period costumes, but it continues to add to the ongoing allure of Hollywood's main man.

Leo, still on a work roll, decided to follow *Mask* with a

cameo appearance in Woody Allen's new film *Celebrity*. His criteria for choosing films is high and Leo was eager at the prospect of working with the legendary Allen. He would be following a slew of actors who have felt similarly. To work with first-class talent has always been appealing to Leo.

As it happens, however, Leo's scenes in the Allen flick, shot over three weeks' time, were with British actor Kenneth Branagh, a first-rate thespian. Leonardo may have signed on for the project thinking he would at least be sharing a little screen time with Woody Allen, but it was not to be. For his *Celebrity* cameo role, Leo is a cocky young Hollywood actor, a stereotype, perhaps.

Hmm. This sounds like a character Leo had portrayed in an experimental film in his not-too-distant past. Several years before, Leo, as a favor to friends, had appeared in a short black-and-white film called *Don's Plum,* directed by R. D. Robb. Leo played the role of a wife-beating drug addict. Also appearing in the film were friends Toby Maguire and Kevin Connelly.

Mostly improvisational, the film features risqué and vulgar dialogue that is allegedly unflattering to Leo. Aware of his image, Leonardo is currently preventing the film from being released, claiming that Robb intends to issue it as a feature of eighty-five minutes, as opposed to the short film (under sixty minutes) it was intended to be. His friend Robb, meanwhile, is suing for $10 million.

Snippets of dialogue were published earlier this year in the *New York Observer*, and they did appear to be rather shocking. One has a hard time imagining these words, bristling with obscenities and vituperative diatribes against women, coming from the world's number one reigning heartthrob.

There's another bit of Leonardo film and dialogue most of us will not get to see or hear. That's because they're from the megastar's commercial debut for Japanese television. Playing a detective, sleekly dressed in all-black, Leonardo bursts into a deluxe Japanese bar, spots the culprit, and immediately fells him with a right hook. A meek waiter then asks in Japanese, "So who's paying the bill, sir?

Leo's reply: "Orico card. Okay?"

Leonardo's paycheck for this slight (fifteen-second) vignette? A whopping $4 million. Hey, give the boy credit, huh? In any case, Leo has certainly come a long way from Matchbox car commercials.

After his phenomenal successes, Leo has said that he wants to take a year off from acting and relax. Hardly. Not a day goes by that the name Leonardo DiCaprio is not spoken, heard, printed, or beamed around the world in one fashion or another. Leo's face is plastered on everything from magazines to TV broadcasts to the Internet to T-shirts. Indeed, "DiCaprio" has been the most searched-for word on Pathfinder, Time Inc.'s Web site, where "Leo" searches are particularly revved up during the 4 P.M. to 8 P.M. hours, when schoolgirls are on the prowl.

As part of the endless fascination with the megastar, there has been much talk of Leonardo's real-estate endeavors. Although it has been written up in more than one publication—from the tabloids to the more respected glossy weeklies—that Leonardo has purchased a million-dollar mansion, Leonardo still lives with his mother and has not yet purchased a house.

He has definitely looked at many properties, including the Spanish-style house in Los Feliz where Heidi Fleiss grew up. That didn't suit him, however, so he then turned

Hollywood Hills Coffee Shop, one of Leo's favorite eateries

his interest to a gorgeous house in the Hollywood Hills. His offer came in too late, which ultimately turned out to be a plus. The manse, it was discovered, was listed in Los Angeles' historic register, and any changes or modifications would have required cutting too much red tape.

Who would have time for that? Not Leonardo DiCaprio, who when he feels like getting away, checks into the hip Chateau Marmont on the Sunset Strip under an assumed name! And don't ask me, because I won't tell!

What will Leo finally choose for his next screen appearance? Many, many irons are in the DiCaprio fire. At various times myriad projects have been bandied about and offered to the star, all hoping to secure the DiCaprio imprimatur. *Slay the Dreamer*, written by Mark Lane and Donald Freed, and inspired by the 1968 assassination of Dr. Martin Luther King, Jr., is one of those projects.

Leonardo is considering playing the lead character, the fictional Jeffrey Jenkins, an eager young lawyer sucked into a confrontation with his powerful father concerning the facts swirling around the assassination.

Leo as a lawyer would certainly be an interesting choice for the hottest man on the planet. Not only would it give him a crack at his first truly contemporary "adult" role, but the actor would be following in the footsteps of Tom Cruise, Chris O'Donnell, and Matt Damon, who have all done very well in legal thrillers.

Leo's father has also been developing a spy drama for Leo based on Julius and Ethel Rosenberg, the husband and wife spy team who were executed in the 1950s. George, who recently met with the Rosenbergs' niece, is also slated to produce under the family company banner, Birken Productions. A father-son DiCaprio production seems to make perfect Hollywood sense. Also on the Birken Productions drawing board, another French role: that of the Marquis de Sade. Leave it to Leo to want to tackle one of history's most colorful characters.

Perhaps one of the most-talked-about films that Leonardo was supposedly attached to is *American Psycho*. Based on the novel by Bret Easton Ellis, it was to be an independent production of Lions Gate Films. The film is about a twenty-six-year-old yuppie serial killer, whose fondness for viciously murdering girls is matched only by his indulgent narcissism and obsession with designer labels.

Splashed across the front pages of the Hollywood trade papers and prominently reported in the *Los Angeles Times,* the announcement of this possibility stunned many in the industry. Young Leo as a grisly serial killer? Talk about a radical image departure!

Even the book's original publisher, Simon and Schuster, had dropped the title from its list when the book and its author were attacked by the Los Angeles chapter of the National Organization for Women and other feminist groups. The book was eventually published by Vintage, a paperback imprint of Random House, but it was certainly no boost, at that time, to Ellis's literary career.

The topper, though? Leo would be paid $21 million, the highest salary an actor to date has received. But how would his fans accept him in this morally repugnant take on the high-flying eighties?

George DiCaprio has stated in no uncertain terms that Leonardo is not doing the picture, nor does he want his son doing the picture. Let's face it: America is not thrilled seeing its screen legends play psychopathic killers. Anthony Hopkins, after all, was not exactly besieged with romantic leads after starring in *The Silence of the Lambs*.

After much ink had been spilled, the news was then revealed that the publicity machine, which had started cranking in high gear at the Cannes International Film Festival earlier this year, had gotten completely out of control and Leonardo had at no time actually committed himself to *American Psycho*.

Leonardo had also been touted to star in an adaptation of Cormac McCarthy's *All the Pretty Horses,* directed by Oscar winner Billy Bob Thornton. When Leo's fee reportedly became too high, Matt Damon was signed on for a "mere" $5 million.

Recently Leo has been in New York, meeting with various directors from Harmony Korine to Oliver Stone to Spike Lee. He has been considering, as one can imagine, numerous projects. Among his choices is a film adaptation of John Irving's *The Cider House Rules,* to be directed by Lasse Hallström, who so deftly guided Leo to an Oscar nomination in his film, *What's Eating Gilbert Grape?*

Whatever Leo ultimately opts to do for his next picture, the brilliant actor is at the top of his game now, and will no doubt be for a long time to come. Judiciously weighing his options, Leonardo is also trying to relax and get in some traveling. He went to Cuba earlier this year with his father and stepmother, taking part in a "cultural exchange."

Leonardo has also been donating a portion of his time to charitable events. As part of the Make-a-Wish Foundation, Leo recently treated eight young girls—all cancer patients—to lunch at Beverly Hills' Planet Hollywood restaurant. Not only did he fête the thrilled teenage girls, he lovingly bestowed kisses on all of them, as well as giving the girls shirts embroidered by his mother, Irmelin.

Whatever Leo chooses to do next to follow up his mega-success, one thing is for certain: Leonardo is scheduled to have knee surgery on a nagging sports injury, one that will require him to undergo nearly three months of physical therapy, accompanied by lots of rest.

Rest?

The young actor, or so it seems, hasn't had much rest since he embarked upon a showbiz career. A good thing for his countless fans, who consider each Leonardo DiCaprio movie a treasure in and of itself. Whatever he chooses next will be perfect, because Leo, who is currently studying yoga to stay focused and centered, has always been one to live in the moment.

And that moment is now.

His heart...and career...will go on!

Love Is Leonardo

BY VICTORIA LOOSELEAF AND
CRAIG URQUHART

© Craig Urquhart and Victoria Looseleaf 1998

Filmography

Critters 3 (1991)
DIRECTED BY: Kristine Peterson
RELEASED BY: New Line Cinema
CAST: Leonardo DiCaprio,
Christopher Cousins,
Joseph Cousins, Don Opper

Poison Ivy (1992)
DIRECTED BY: Katt Shea Ruben
PRODUCED BY: Andy Ruben
SCREENPLAY BY: Katt Shea
Ruben, Andy Ruben
MUSIC BY: Aaron Davies
RELEASED BY: New Line Cinema
CAST: Sara Gilbert, Drew
Barrymore, Tom Skerritt,
Cheryl Ladd, Leonardo
DiCaprio

This Boy's Life (1993)
DIRECTED BY: Michael
Caton-Jones
PRODUCED BY: Art Linson
SCREENPLAY BY: Robert Getchell
DIRECTOR OF PHOTOGRAPHY:
David Watkin
BASED ON THE BOOK BY:
Tobias Wolff
MUSIC BY: Carter Burwell
RELEASED BY: Warner Bros.
CAST: Robert De Niro, Ellen

Barkin, Leonardo DiCaprio,
Jonah Blechman

What's Eating Gilbert Grape? (1994)
DIRECTED BY: Lasse Hallström
PRODUCED BY: Meir Teper,
Bertil Ohlsson, David
Matalon
SCREENPLAY BY: Peter Hedges,
based on his novel
DIRECTOR OF PHOTOGRAPHY:
Sven Nykvist, A.S.C.
MUSIC BY: Alan Parker,
Bjorn Isfalt
RELEASED BY: Paramount
Pictures
CAST: Johnny Depp, Leonardo
DiCaprio, Juliette Lewis,
Mary Steenburgen, Darlene
Cates, Laura Harrington,
Mary Kate Schellhardt,
Kevin Tighe

The Foot Shooting Party
(1994)
DIRECTED BY: Annette
Haywood-Carter
SCREENPLAY BY:
Kenneth F. Carter
RELEASED BY: Touchstone
Pictures
CAST: Leonardo DiCaprio

The Quick and the Dead
(1995)
> DIRECTED BY: Sam Raimi
> PRODUCED BY: Joshua Donen,
> Allen Shapiro, Patrick
> Markey
> COPRODUCED BY: Sharon Stone,
> Chuck Binder
> WRITTEN BY: Simon Moore,
> John Sayles (uncredited)
> DIRECTOR OF PHOTOGRAPHY:
> Dante Spinotti
> MUSIC BY: Alan Silvestri
> RELEASED BY: TriStar Pictures
> CAST: Sharon Stone, Gene
> Hackman, Russell Crowe,
> Leonardo DiCaprio, Kevin
> Conway, Gary Sinise

The Basketball Diaries
(1995)
> DIRECTED BY: Scott Kalvert
> PRODUCED BY: Liz Heller, John
> Bard Manulis
> SCREENPLAY BY: Bryan Goluboff
> BASED ON THE BOOK BY: Jim
> Carroll
> MUSIC BY: Graeme Revell
> RELEASED BY: New Line Cinema
> CAST: Leonardo DiCaprio,
> Lorraine Bracco, Mark
> Wahlberg, James Madio,
> Patrick McGaw, Bruno
> Kirby, Ernie Hudson,
> Juliette Lewis, Michael
> Rapaport

Total Eclipse (1995)
> DIRECTED BY: Agnieszka
> Holland
> PRODUCED BY: Jeane-Pierre
> Ramsay Levi
> SCREENPLAY BY: Christopher
> Hampton
> DIRECTOR OF PHOTOGRAPHY:
> Yorgos Arvanitis
> MUSIC BY: Jan A.P. Kaczmarek
> RELEASED BY: Fine Line
> Features
> CAST: Leonardo DiCaprio,
> David Thewlis, Romane
> Bohringer, Dominique
> Blanc, Nita Klein, James
> Thieree, Emmanuelle Oppo

William Shakespeare's Romeo & Juliet (1996)
> DIRECTED BY: Baz Luhrmann
> PRODUCED BY: Gabriella
> Martinelli, Baz Luhrmann
> SCREENPLAY BY: Craig Pearce,
> Baz Luhrmann
> DIRECTOR OF PHOTOGRAPHY:
> Donald M. McAlpine, A.S.C.
> MUSIC BY: Nellee Hooper
> RELEASED BY: 20th Century Fox
> CAST: Leonardo DiCaprio,
> Claire Danes, John
> Leguizamo, Paul Sorvino,
> Brian Dennehy, Christina
> Pickles, Paul Rudd, Diane
> Venora, Harold Perrineau,

Des'ree, Peter
Postlethwaite, Pedro
Altamirano

Marvin's Room (1996)
DIRECTED BY: Jerry Zaks
PRODUCED BY: Robert De Niro,
Jane Rosenthal, Scott
Rudin, Adam Schroeder
BASED ON THE PLAY BY: Scott
McPherson
RELEASED BY: Miramax Films
CAST: Leonardo DiCaprio,
Meryl Streep, Diane
Keaton, Robert De Niro,
Hume Cronyn, Gwen
Verdon

Titanic (1997)
DIRECTED BY: James Cameron
PRODUCED BY: James Cameron,
Jon Landau, Rae Sanchini
SCREENPLAY BY: James Cameron
RELEASED BY: 20th Century
Fox/Paramount Pictures
CAST: Leonardo DiCaprio,
Kate Winslet, Billy Zane,
Kathy Bates, Bill Paxton,
Gloria Stuart, Frances
Fisher

The Man in the Iron Mask
(1998)
DIRECTED BY: Randall Wallace
PRODUCED BY: Randall Wallace,

Russ Smith, Rene Dupont
SCREENPLAY BY: Randall Wallace
INSPIRED BY THE FRENCH NOVEL BY:
Alexandre Dumas
DIRECTED OF PHOTOGRAPHY: Peter
Suschitzky
COSTUME DESIGNER: James
Acheson
RELEASED BY: United Artists
CAST: Leonardo DiCaprio,
Jeremy Irons, John
Malkovich, Gerard
Depardieu, Gabriel Byrne,
Anne Parillaud, Judith
Godreche

Celebrity (1998)
DIRECTED BY: Woody Allen
SCREENPLAY BY: Woody Allen
CAST: Woody Allen, Kenneth
Branagh, Judy Davis,
Leonardo DiCaprio,
Melanie Griffith, Joe
Mantegna, Irina Pantaeva,
Winona Ryder, Jeffrey
Wright

the LOOSELEAF

REPORT

For more information about Leo,
contact Victoria Looseleaf at

**The Looseleaf Report, Inc.
Box 10356
Beverly Hills, CA 90213-3356**

Or call 1-800-251-2252

And visit the author's Web site at
www.looseleafreport.com